Japanese Sword Drawing

apanese Sword Drawing

A Source Book for Iaido Students

By Don J. Zier

日本居合

UP **UNIQUE PUBLICATIONS**
Burbank, California

Disclaimer

Please note that the author and publisher of this book are NOT RESPONSIBLE in any manner whatsoever for any injury that may result from practicing the techniques and/or following the instructions given within. Since the physical activities described herein may be too strenuous in nature for some readers to engage in safely, it is essential that a physician be consulted prior to training.

First published in 2000 by Unique Publications.

Library of Congress Catalog Number: 2001 131324
ISBN: 0-86568-162-7

Unique Publications
4201 Vanowen Place
Burbank, CA 91505
(800) 332–3330

First edition

05 04 03 02 01 00 99 98 97 1 3 5 7 9 10 8 6 4 2

Printed in the United States of America

Contents

PART THREE: Established Kata of the Japanese Federations

APPENDIX

Foreword
The Students' Perspective

This book presents many technical details of *Muso Shinden Ryu Iaido*, making this a useful guide for sword drawing teachers and students. One aspect of instruction that is not covered, however, is *how* the art is taught. As long-time students of the author (that's us in the pictures), we wanted to comment on the instruction we received, thus shedding some light on that aspect of the art. In addition to being a sort of tribute to Don, for whom we both have great affection, we believe that much of the value we continue to derive from *iaido* comes as much from the *way* he taught as from *what* he taught.

From our first class, it was apparent that Don was technically proficient in *iaido*. He was teaching something that he knew how to do, and do well. As he had completed his formal instruction in *iaido* some years before we began studying with him, his skill was obvious and gave us something to aspire to. It was not just the flash of a blade that inspired us. He made us wait until we held black belts in another martial art before agreeing to teach us (so he wouldn't have to start *completely* from scratch)—and by then we knew the difference between flash and substance.

Don also has a thorough understanding of the art. He knows the difference between the correct movements and similar-but-incorrect ones and is able to demonstrate these differences. Unlike traditional instruction, which is largely based on imitation, our instruction was based on analysis, explanation, and illustration. Rather than trying to duplicate an entire form, we spent considerable time practicing individual movements within a specific form. For example, we learned that a single, gross movement, such as the overhead cut (*shomen uchi*), can be produced in several ways—some strong and others not. By breaking each form into its component movements, Don built the form from the "inside out." Thus, when the component movements were mastered, the rest was easy. This process was the essence of our instruction.

As you might imagine, we spent most or our time learning and refining basic movements. We practiced with wooden swords (*boken*) for three years before drawing with bladed ones. We spent ten years on the twelve *Omori Ryu* forms and learned the remaining forms in about two years. That we did not get bored in these years is a tribute to the detail and interest with which we were instructed. (Although Don probably felt safer when we trained with *boken*, live blades require the use of a scabbard, which adds yet one more thing to move at the right time, in the right direction, and at the right speed. He was simply waiting until we were ready for "advanced" techniques. Or maybe we were just slow learners.)

The result of our instruction is that we are *different* because of it. We move and think differently than when we began; we are not just the same people who now also do *iaido*. Don would be the first to say that his approach to teaching *iaido* is not traditional. But he has never claimed any legitimacy on the grounds of tradition, only on performance. His instruction has been among the more gratifying experiences we have had, and we are pleased that he has *finally* finished this book so that others might appreciate it as well.

—Tom Lang & Rich Radcliffe

Part One

Preliminaries

1. Overview

BACKGROUND

Iaido (the way of sword drawing) is one of the more formal Japanese *budo* (martial ways). This formality appears in the manner of practice, philosophical underpinnings, and origins of the various systems. The training is very rigid, and there is a corresponding lack of "free practice."

Sword drawing practice is usually done in a place designated especially for it. Participants wear traditional Japanese martial art uniforms: a *keikogi* or *juban* (light jacket) on the upper body, closed with an *obi* (wide belt), and *hakama* (wide trousers) on the lower body. The jacket should fit well, not too loosely; the belt should go around the body three times with enough extra length to tie in a knot in the back; the trousers should come to the ankles. Practice is done with traditional weapons: the *boken* or *bokuto* (wooden sword), the *iaito* (practice sword), and *katana* (actual sword).

The sword used in practice, whether wooden or steel, is worn in *bukezukuri* (the warrior method). The scabbard is placed between the second and third layers of the belt, edge-up. If a second, or short sword is also worn, its scabbard is inserted between the first and second layers, also edge up. The short sword's guard and the long sword's hilt are both n line with the navel. Both scabbards point to the left.

Photo 1: front view, standing, *bukezukuri*

Photo 2: left side view, standing, *bukezukuri*

3

Placing the scabbards between different layers of the belt prevents them from touching and protects the scabbards from bodily oils and sweat.

Iaido practice itself is carried out in a formal manner. The positions of the *kata* (forms) were those of Japanese life, even if some are no longer common. Various bows are performed during the course of practice.

The philosophy which is most often expounded in sword drawing schools is of relatively recent origin. The records that exist of very old systems show a philosophy heavily influenced by Taoism. The more modern systems are more closely aligned with Zen Buddhism; Zen itself was, of course, influenced by Taoism in its seminal phases.

The forms practiced in sword drawing (which vary from system to system) are intended to be practiced for their own sake, rather than for any consideration of "combat effectiveness." The movements are designed to train the practitioner in "internalizing." That is, in immersing oneself into the form to such an extent that individual characteristics fall away. The form can be said to exist independently, manifesting itself through the practitioner.

Sword drawing practice, like that of other Japanese martial ways, passes through three sequential phases. In the first phase, *shu* (keeping), the practitioner copies his instructor, memorizing the forms. In the second phase, *ha* (breaking), the practitioner seeks to analyze and understand the movements of the forms. In the third phase, *ri* (leaving), the practitioner seeks to understand the essence of the forms and to arrive at an impersonal practice. These phases also characterize a gradually attenuating relationship between teacher and student.

It should be noted that the application of phased instruction does not always work well with Western students.

There are many systems of sword drawing. Several have existed for more than seventeen generations—the most successful of which are still practiced today, while the least successful are only historical curiosities.

The system documented in this work, *Muso Shinden Ryu*, has its roots in the teaching of Hayashi Jinsuke Shigenobu (c. 1543 –1621). He founded the *Shinmei Muso Ryu* system in the late 16th century. Since that time, the teachings have passed through a succession of headmasters, resulting in the system's name and forms being altered a number of times. The headmaster lineage of *Muso Shinden Ryu* is diagrammed in the Appendix.

Around the year 1800, a major split in this lineage occurred, giving rise to two main schools of sword drawing. One of these eventually became the *Muso Jikiden Eishin Ryu*; the other, *Muso Shinden Ryu*. The last headmaster of the *Muso Shinden Ryu*, Nakayama Hakudo, attempted a reconciliation between the two branches by studying the forms of the *Jikiden Ryu*. He formalized the *Muso Shinden Ryu*'s current structure and content after this study, in around 1923.

夢想神伝流居合道

Muso Shinden Ryu

Nakayama died in 1958, and since then no one has been named headmaster to the *Muso Shinden Ryu*.

Japanese sword drawing, which is studied outside of a particular system (e.g., the *Muso Shinden Ryu*) is organized into two main administrative groups. These are the *Zen Nihon Iaido Renmei* (the All-Japan Sword Drawing Federation), and the *Zen Nihon Kendo Renmei* (the All-Japan Fencing Federation). Most sword drawing practitioners belong to one or the other federation. However, some of the traditional systems maintain independent schools and instruction. Of course, the quality of practice varies widely, as does the quality of instruction.

Sword drawing instruction in the United States is mostly found in schools teaching *kendo* (Japanese fencing), or in other schools where sword drawing is an adjunct to the martial arts normally taught. These schools often rank practitioners in their own sword drawing forms. The ranks are sometimes recognized within affiliate schools, but other systems often do not recognize them. The ranks with the widest acceptance seem to be those given by the American Iaido Federation, affiliated with the American Kendo Federation, headquartered in Los Angeles.

SCOPE

The intent of this book is to record—and thus being a resource to sword drawing practitioners—the forms that are orally taught in a sword drawing class.

The information in this work documents the three styles of sword drawing taught in the *Muso Shinden Ryu* (Traditional Spiritual Vision System) of sword drawing. These styles, or traditions, are called *Shoden* (the First Tradition), *Chuden* (the Middle Tradition), and *Okuden* (the Inner Tradition). Each of these is actually a system of sword drawing in its own right and will be discussed in detail in Part Two of this work.

In addition, the *Seitei Kata* (Official Forms) of the All-Japan Fencing Federation and the All-Japan Sword Drawing Federation are described in Part Three.

Japanese writing uses three styles: *kaisho* (the printed style), *gyosho* (the semi-cursive style), and *sosho* (the cursive style). Each of these is progressively harder to write (and read); mastery of each forms the foundation of the next. The Japanese believe that progression through these styles of writing cannot be done on technical skill alone, but requires an internal esthetic development.

The three traditions of the *Muso Shinden Ryu* correspond to the three styles of writing. Accordingly, practitioners must have firmly mastered each tradition before going on to the next.

Recording the forms of a system should not be confused with transmitting its traditions. And as this work merely represents resource material, it does not transmit the traditions of the *Muso Shinden Ryu*.

In addition, as described above, *Muso Shinden Ryu* has a companion system, the *Muso Jikiden Eishin Ryu*. The forms of this system are also divided into a three-tiered structure, and often have the same names. They are quite distinct, however, and the reader should be well aware that this is often a source of confusion. Thus, this work also does not document the traditions of the *Jikiden Ryu*, its techniques, or the differences between it and the *Muso Shinden Ryu*.

CONVENTIONS

In describing sword drawing forms in print, which is a difficult task at best, certain conventions will be used. First, the form will be generally described. This description will contain the rationale for the actions of the form and describe the position and movements of the imaginary enemy(ies). Next, a commentary will discuss the salient features of the form. Then the actual movements of the form will be described in sequence; simultaneous movements will be indicated by the use of "bullets" (•). Comments concerning important aspects of the movements will follow.

Certain terms will also be used to describe the sword. The blade, unless otherwise noted, will refer to the edge. The normal sheathed position is blade-vertical, edge-upward. After being drawn, when held in both hands, the blade is vertical, edge downward. When the sword is held horizontally, the edge will usually face away from the body.

The forms are demonstrated so that the main action directly faces the viewer. This means that if the form contains a pivot before the main action, the practitioner must take his seat so that the pivot will place him facing the viewer.

In the descriptions of the forms, the viewer's direction is denoted as the "front." The practitioner will be directed where to sit in relation to the "front."

At the first use of any significant sword drawing term or phrase, the Romanization of the Japanese will be given, using the Hepburn system, followed by the translation in parentheses. After this, the English translation will normally be used; only proper names will continue to be given in Romanized Japanese.

The reader should be aware that written Japanese is often different than the spoken language, wherein many written syllables are unvoiced. Where the pronunciation of terms differs in this fashion, a guide will be given in quotation marks.

2. Basic Techniques

Iaido forms begin from either a standing or sitting position, of which there are two sitting positions. The first, *seiza* (straight sitting), is described in the preliminary section of Chapter 3. The second, *tate hiza* (drawn-up knee sitting), will be discussed in the preliminary section of Chapter 4. *Seiza* is considered the more formal of the two seated positions, and is still used in daily Japanese life.

When standing, the sword is usually held with both hands. There are five classical postures for doing this. In the basic position, *chudan* (the middle position), the sword is extended to the center front, pointing at the eyes of the imaginary opponent.

Photo 1: front view, standing, *chudan*

Photo 2: left side view, standing, *chudan*

The sword point is dropped, to point toward the opponent's knees, in a more passive position called *gedan* (the low position).

Photo 3: front view, standing, *gedan*

Photo 4: left side view, standing, *gedan*

7

The sword is held overhead in an aggressive position called *jodan* (the high position). This posture can be taken with either the left or right foot forward.

Photo 5: front view, standing, *jodan*

Photo 6: left side view, standing, *jodan*

The aggression displayed in the high position can be softened to an alert watchfulness displayed in *hasso no gamae* (the eight-phased position). Here the sword is held in front of the right shoulder, with the blade vertical and the sword-guard in line with the mouth.

Photo 7: front view, standing,
hasso no gamae

Photo 8: right side view, standing,
hasso no gamae

The fifth position, the most passive of all, is *waka no gamae* (the side position). The sword is turned to the rear along the right side, pointing downward.

Photo 9: front view, standing, *waka no gamae*

Photo 10: right side view, standing, *waka no gamae*

The basic actions of any sword drawing form can be classified into one of four categories: *nuki tsuke* (drawing); *kiritsuke* (cutting); *chiburi* (blood-cleaning); and *noto* (sheathing). As a preliminary, we will examine each of these categories separately. Each of the following sections discusses a standing technique. The reader should be aware that any of these may also be executed from either of the sitting positions.

DRAWING

The draw is intended not only to bring the sword quickly into play, but also to inflict injury on the enemy. Japanese sword drawing is not the same as fencing, with its tacit give-and-take between opponents. The techniques preserved in the sword drawing forms are the immediate and aggressive fighting actions of a determined warrior. The practitioner must realize this by manifesting *seme* (attacking) when demonstrating the forms.

Three draws are common: a vertical draw (in which the sword is drawn as it is, with the edge upward); a horizontal draw (in which the sword is given a quarter turn to the left and drawn with the edge facing horizontally to the left); and an underhand draw (in which the sword is fully turned over and drawn with the edge downward. Only the first two draws appear in the various forms comprising the *Muso Shinden Ryu*. An example of the underhand draw can be found in the third form described in Chapter 8.

Whether sitting or standing, the draw is accompanied by foot movement. In general, the draw is started when the left foot is forward of, or at least even with, the right foot; the draw is completed, and the attack made on the enemy, when the right foot is in front. This usually involves a forward right step, but occasionally the left foot pulls backwards. There are, however, exceptions to this rule. The descriptions of the forms will note these.

The sword is not pulled from the scabbard, but pushed. That is, the right hand does not pass around the stomach, approaching the grip from the hilt and then drawing by retracing this path. The right hand slides directly across the stomach, taking the grip just behind the sword guard and then pushing the hilt (butt-first) outward. The elbow stays behind the hand, which not only protects it from an enemy's strike, but allows maximum force in the draw-and-strike which follows.

Horizontal Draw

Face the front.
You are standing, facing your enemy, who is assumed to be 1.5 meters away.

To compose yourself, take three breaths.
These three breaths will be done at the beginning of all the forms as psychological preparation.

Photo 11: front view, standing, *bukezukuri*

With the commencement of the third breath place both hands on the sword.
Grasp the scabbard with the left hand. Grip the hilt with the right hand, thumb underneath. Keep the right fingers loose.

Photo 12: front view, initiating standing horizontal draw

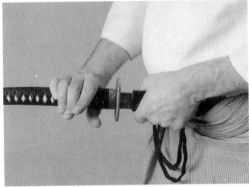

Photo 13: left side closeup of hands

Slowly draw the sword, with the blade facing upward.

Photo 14: front view, draw to turnover   Photo 15: left side view, draw to turnover

When the sword has been drawn to within 10cm of its point, deliberately turn the blade and scabbard to the horizontal, edge to the outside.

The scabbard is turned over by the left hand, not the right. The hilt rotates in the right hand so that the thumb is now on the side. The sword travels about 1cm during this turn.

Photo 16: front view, draw after turnover   Photo 17: left side view, draw after turnover

Advance the right foot one step to the front. The left hand, grasping the scabbard mouth (the scabbard is horizontal at this time), frees the point by drawing the scabbard backward. While you do this, suddenly draw the remaining 9cm of the blade, striking the enemy's chest or temple.

When doing this, feel as though the left elbow is attached to the scabbard. The

scabbard moves to the rear side in one stroke. The movement pulls the left shoulder to the rear. Continue to look squarely to the front.

At the completion of the draw the right fist is about the same height as the right shoulder. The sword point is directly in front of the body and may hang down a little. This is described as follows: if water were to begin flowing from the handguard, it would flow gently to the sword point. This is a small formality called sui hashiri (running water).

Photo 18: front view, standing,
end of horizontal draw

Photo 19: left side view, standing,
end of horizontal draw

Vertical Draw

Photo 20: front view, standing, *bukezukuri*

Face the front.
> *You are standing, facing your enemy, who is assumed to be 1.5 meters away.*

To compose yourself, take three breaths.
> *These three breaths will be done at the beginning of all the forms as psychological preparation.*

With the commencement of the third breath, place both hands on the sword. *Grasp the scabbard with the left hand. Grip the hilt with the right hand more deeply, pushing the thumb up along the side of the hilt from underneath. Keep the right fingers loose.*

Photo 21: front view, initiating
standing vertical draw

Photo 22: left side closeup of hands

Slowly draw the sword, with the blade facing upward. *The left hand raises the scabbard mouth until it points up about 60 degrees, then draws the scabbard down along the blade. The right hand draws the sword along the natural curve of the blade. The scabbard must not bind the draw. The point emerges in a natural fashion.*

Photo 23: front view, draw to release

Photo 24: left side view, draw to release

Allow the point to swing around the left shoulder until it is to the rear.

Photo 25: left side view, sword passing
left shoulder

Photo 26: left side view, sword passing
left shoulder

Advance the right foot one step to
the front.

Cut downward at the enemy from
this high position.

Photo 27: left side view, standing,
one-handed downward cut

CUTTING

Although the initial draw is expected to injure the enemy, it is often not forceful
enough to kill him. The form must demonstrate additional techniques to accomplish this. Most of these fall into the category of cutting.

The cut most often used is a two-handed, overhead cut to the center front.
Sometimes this cut is varied by a slanting delivery, intended to cut the right or left
side of the enemy's head or upper body. The mechanics of these cuts are essentially the same.

Although the cut may appear to be the same movement as the cut used in Japanese fencing, it is not. The fencing cut is more of a "rap," designed to allow the fencer to rebound into follow-up techniques. The sword drawing cut is intended to inflict as much harm on the enemy as possible, thus it must be much more powerful.

Vertical Cut

Having drawn the sword, swing the sword overhead by stabbing the point to the rear, passing about 10cm above and outside the left shoulder. Move the left foot forward up to the right heel.

Draw the scabbard back around until the mouth reaches the vicinity of the stomach. Then release the scabbard and grasp the hilt with the left hand, on its way overhead.

Make sure the sword guard does not cross the center line.

This is called to o furi kamuri *(swinging the sword overhead). The movement draws the scabbard mouth in line with the center, so that the scabbard does not hinder the cut. Splay your elbows as you raise your arms.*

Photo 28: front view, standing, end of horizontal draw

Photo 29: left side view, standing, end of horizontal draw

Photo 30: front view, sword over left shoulder

Photo 31: left side view,
sword over left shoulder

Photo 32: front closeup
of left hand on scabbard

Photo 33: front view, *jodan*

Photo 34: left side view, *jodan*

Stamp the right foot down again one step forward. Cut downward at the center of the enemy's head.

Swing your arms down sharply to complete the strike. As your arms swing down, eliminate the splay of your elbows by extending your arms and by "wringing" the hilt with your hands. This puts your wrists behind the sword so they can withstand the impact of the cut.

Your left arm powers the cut and swings down as it extends. Your right arm directs the cut and pushes forward as it extends. The cut stops naturally when your right arm is fully extended.

Be aware of a single flowing movement from the overhead swing to the downward cut. This is called i hyoshi no uchi *(the strike of one rhythm).*

Photo 35: front view, standing, downward cut

Photo 36: left side view, standing, downward cut

Photo 37: left side view, downward cut w/ overlay showing arcs and centers

BLOOD-CLEANING

Blood-cleaning is the largely symbolic action of removing the enemy's blood from the blade. There are several types of cleanings used in the *Muso Shinden Ryu* forms. The following are the two most common.

Omori ryu no chiburi (Blood-cleaning of the Omori Ryu)

Photo 38: front view, *chudan*

Having a two-handed grip on the sword, hold it in a middle position, about waist level.

This is chudan, *the basic fencing position. The right foot is forward.*

Remove the left hand from the hilt and place it, palm open, on the scabbard at the left waist. The right hand extends, stretching out the elbow, raising the sword to the right side.

The height of the right fist is about the same as the right shoulder. The sword tip points about 60 degrees to the rear.

Photo 39: front view, sword extended to right

Photo 40: front closeup, left hand

Photo 41: front view, sword extended to rear

Bend the right elbow, bringing the right fist toward the right temple.

Photo 42: front view, sword approaching head

Just as the elbow makes a 45-degree angle, swing the sword sharply down in front of the body.
   The right fingertips pass near the face.

Photo 43: front view, sword passing face

Photo 44: front view,
end of standing *omori chiburi*

The sword point comes cleanly to the low, right, diagonal side of the body.
When swinging the sword downwards, make a forceful, but not showy effort. Done correctly, the little and middle fingers accelerate the sword point. The downward swing of the sword sends the tip out in front parallel to the tip of the foot.

Eishin ryu no chiburi (Blood-Cleaning of the Eishin Ryu)

Photo 45: front view, *chudan*

Having a two-handed grip on the sword, hold it in a middle position, about waist level.
This is chudan, *the basic fencing position. The right foot is forward.*

Remove the left hand from the hilt and place it, palm open, on the scabbard at the left waist. The right hand retains its grasp, and the right arm opens to the right side, ending with a slight snap as the elbow straightens.
The sword assumes a downward diagonal position, much as before, but without the large swing. It is important to center the action on the right elbow, not the right hand.

Photo 46: front view,
sword moving to right side

Photo 47: left closeup, left hand

Photo 48: front view,
end of standing *eishin chiburi*

SHEATHING

Sheathing is the act of returning the sword to the scabbard. The decision to sheath assumes that an action is complete and that the warrior is victorious. Nevertheless, the warrior is ever on guard, so the sheathing must be done with *zan shin* (remaining heart). In most forms this is demonstrated by the contrast in speed between the first part of the sheathing and the last. Following is a general description of the most common sheathing action.

With the hips held firm, grasp the scabbard mouth with the left hand, twist it to the horizontal. Swing up the sword to rest on the left hand, edge horizontal.

Rest the back of the sword in the neighborhood of the handguard in the hollow of the index finger and the thumb.

Photo 49: front view, end of standing
omori chiburi

Photo 50: front view, scabbard turned

Photo 51: front closeup, left hand

Photo 52: front view, sword on left hand

Photo 53: front closeup, hilt

Photo 54: front view, *noto* to point entry

Draw the right hand quickly out to the right front, stretching out the elbow, until the sword point reaches the scabbard mouth. The left hand withdraws the scabbard a little.

The sword moves to the side in one stroke. Do not drop the point. Do not look. The motion of the two hands meet at the end of sheathing.

Insert the sword point in the scabbard mouth with the left hand.

Photo 55: front closeup, point entry

Slide the blade, horizontally into the scabbard.

Photo 56: front view,
blade inserted to turnover

Photo 57: left side view,
blade inserted to turnover

When you have inserted two-thirds of the blade, deliberately turn the blade upward and insert the remainder vertically and much more slowly.

Photo 58: front view, blade after turnover

Photo 59: left side view, blade after turnover

Photo 60: front view, end of standing *noto*

Part Two

The Traditional Schools of Jaido

3. The First Tradition: Omori Ryu

BACKGROUND

The *Omori Ryu* (The Big Forest System) is a style of traditional sword drawing. It is currently taught as the First Tradition of the *Muso Shinden Ryu*. As such, it is regarded as the most approachable of the three styles that compose this system.

Omori Ryu contains eleven forms (plus a spare one). All but one of these begin from *seiza*, the more formal seated posture. The forms are designated by name as well as number. Sometimes a second title is given, usually more descriptive than the first. The eleven forms are named as follows:

Shohatto (Initial Sword); *mae* (front)

Sa To (Following Sword); *hidari* (left)

U To (Right Sword); *migi* (right)

Atari To (Striking Sword); *ushiro* (rear)

Inyo Shintai (Advancing-Retreating Movement);
yae gaki (doubled fences)

Ryu To (Flowing Sword); *ukenagashi* (parrying)

Jun To (Obedient Sword); *kaishaku* (assistant at suicide)

Gyaku To (Reversed Sword); *tsukekomi* (take advantage of)

Seichu To (Center-Strengthened Sword); *tsukikage* (moonlight)

Koran To (Tiger-Fighting Sword); *oikaze* (pursuing wind)

Nuki Uchi (Sudden Attack); *nuki uchi* (drawing strike)

In addition to the above eleven forms, a twelfth "spare" form is practiced. This form is sometimes used to replace number five, *Inyo Shintai*, and is titled **Inyo Shintai Kaewaza** (advancing-retreating movement, alternate technique).

PRELIMINARIES

As eleven of the forms begin in the *seiza* posture. Accordingly, the first preliminary matter is to describe the taking, and leaving, of this position.

Sitting in *Seiza*

Stand with the feet together.

Photo 1: front view, standing

Draw the left foot back about one half step, until the toes adjoin the right instep. *The left heel rises off the floor.*

Photo 2: front view, foot drawn back

Photo 3: left side closeup, feet

Begin to kneel vertically, keeping the back straight.

Try to bring the left buttock to the left heel. The toes stay bent under.

Photo 4: front view, dropped to heel

When you have dropped as far as possible, gently tip the left knee forward and down onto the floor.

The right knee will still be up in the air.

Photo 5: front view, left knee on floor

Then gently tip the right knee to the floor.

The right knee will be ahead of the left.

Draw the right knee back to make the knees even, about two fists apart.

Photo 6: front view, both knees on floor

Straighten the toes so they point to
the rear and bring them together,
left big toe on top of the right.

Photo 7: rear closeup, feet

Sit on your heels.
> *If you practice this, the steps will
> blend to a single movement. The
> pleated front of the trousers will
> fold naturally under your knees
> and not require any manual
> adjustment.*

Photo 8: front view, *seiza*

Photo 9: left side view, *seiza*

Rising from *Seiza*

Sitting formally, rise to both knees. At the top of the rise, turn the toes of both feet
under. Raise the right knee from the floor and advance the right foot about one
half step.
> *If you have been sitting properly, the trousers will not impede the feet.*
> > *The toes stay under.*

Photo 10: front view, *seiza*

Photo 11: left side view, *seiza*

Photo 12: front view, kneeling on both knees

Photo 13: rear closeup, toes

Photo 14: front view, right knee up

Gently rock backwards to bring the left knee off the floor.

Keep the back vertical. The left buttock should rest on the left heel.

Rise vertically from this position to standing.

Bring the left foot forward and make the feet even.

Photo 15: front view, standing

This is the *Ogasawara* style of sitting, which is the most formal. Some sword drawing schools do not use this, but use a more informal method. In this case, the left foot is carried backwards a full step and the body is lowered to the left knee. The right knee is placed on the floor, the feet are made even and the body is lowered to the sitting position.

Since this simpler method does not preserve the folds in the wide trousers, before sitting strike the insides of each trouser leg with the right hand. This sweeps the trouser legs backwards and away and prevents them from interfering with subsequent movements.

The practice of sword drawing is quite formal. Although the actual practices differ from system to system, almost all show respect by bowing. In all cases, some formality is used when first inserting the sword into the belt, and when last removing it. The following is a general description of such a formality.

BEGINNING FORMALITY

The sword is carried to the practice area in the right hand, with the hilt to the rear and the edge downward. Any cords are tied around the scabbard.

Perform a standing bow upon entry to the practice area.

Photo 16: front view, sword in right hand

Photo 17: right side view, sword in right hand

Pass the sword to the front and transfer it to the left hand, carrying it with the hilt forward, edge up, with the thumb over the guard.

Advance to the spot where the sword-insertion is to take place.

Lower the body to *seiza*.

Place the sword on the ground, edge to the outside, guard in line with the left knee.

Remove the left hand.

Photo 18: front view, middle of pass

Photo 19: front closeup, hands

Photo 20: front view, sword in left hand

Photo 21: left side view, sword in left hand

Photo 22: front view, *seiza,*
w/ sword on left side ground

Photo 23: left side view, *seiza,*
w/ sword on left side ground

If there are any bows to perform to the instructor or others, do so now.

Photo 24: front view, sword raised in left hand

Resume the grip on the sword.

Lift the sword to the front until the guard is centered, chest high, with the scabbard hanging diagonally down to the left.

Grip the sword with the right hand, palm under the guard.

Slide the left hand, palm down, to the butt, lifting the sword to horizontal.

Photo 25: front view, right hand on sword

Photo 26: front closeup, hands

Photo 27: front view, sword horizontal

Photo 28: front view,
left hand standing sword vertical

If there are cords, use the left hand to stand the sword vertically in front of the right knee, edge to the left.

Use the left hand to rotate the scabbard 180 degrees, edge to the right.

Photo 29: front view, rotated scabbard

Photo 30: front closeup, hands

Photo 31: front view,
left hand drawing out cords

Use the left hand to unfasten the cords, drawing them horizontally to the left to straighten out any kinks.

Photo 32: front view, left hand lowering cords

Let the cords hang down the scabbard.

Use the left hand to again rotate the scabbard 180-degrees, edge to the left.

Photo 33: front view, rotated scabbard

Photo 34: front closeup, hands

Photo 35: front view,
left hand grasping scabbard

Grasp the scabbard and cords together with the left hand and bring the sword back to the high horizontal position from which you started.

Photo 36: front view, sword horizontal

Place the sword on the floor in front, with the guard in line with the right knee, and the edge away from you.

Arrange any cords parallel to the scabbard.

Perform the seated bow.
This is called the to rei *(sword bow).*

Photo 37: front view, sword placed on floor

Photo 38: front view, *seiza,*
w/ sword on ground in front

If there are cords, pick them up with the little fingers of the right hand.

Photo 39: front view,
right hand picking up cords

Photo 40: front view, sword horizontal

Re-grip the sword as above and raise it again to horizontal.

Rotate the sword in the right hand until you can insert the left thumb into the belt at the center waist, between the second and third layers.

Use the left hand to insert the butt into the belt.

Photo 41: front view, sword inserted in *obi*

Photo 42: left side view, sword inserted in *obi*

As the scabbard emerges from the belt through the left side opening of the wide trousers, slide the left hand to the butt and draw the sword fully to the rear.

Photo 43: front view, left hand
drawing sword to rear

Photo 44: left side view, left hand
drawing sword to rear

Slide the left hand up the scabbard and grasp the sword at the guard. Release the right hand.

Photo 45: front view, *seiza,* w/ sword settled, cords in right hand

Photo 46: left side view, *seiza,* w/ sword settled, cords in right hand

Photo 47: front view, drawing cords to right

If there are cords, draw them to the right and tie them around the trouser strings at the right side opening.

Photo 48: front view, tying knot

Photo 49: front closeup, tying knot

Rest the right hand on the right thigh.

Release the left hand and rest it on the left thigh.

Stand and move to the waiting area or directly to the practice position.

Photo 50: front closeup, tying knot

ENDING FORMALITY

Advance to the spot where the sword-removal is to take place, with the sword correctly placed in the belt.

Photo 51: front view, *seiza,* w/ sword settled

Grip the sword with the left hand, thumb over the guard.

Lower the body to *seiza.*

Photo 52: front view, *seiza,* w/ sword settled

Photo 53: left side view, *seiza* w/ sword settled

Photo 54: front view, drawing cords to right

If there are cords, untie them and hold the ends with the little fingers of the right hand.

Begin to draw the scabbard forward out of the belt with the left hand.

Photo 55: front view, right hand on sword

When the left hand is advanced about 10cm. grip the handle with the right hand as before, palm underneath.

Continue advancing the sword, but restrain the left hand from moving forward.

Photo 56: front view, right hand
withdrawing scabbard

Photo 57: left side view, right hand
withdrawing scabbard

As the butt emerges from the belt, grasp it with the left hand, palm on top.

Photo 58: front view, left hand on sword

Bring the sword up to the horizontal.

Photo 59: front view, sword horizontal

If there are cords being held by the right fingers, use the left hand to stand the sword vertically in front of the right knee, edge to the left.

Photo 60: front view, left hand
standing sword vertical

Use the left hand to rotate the sword 180-degrees, edge to the right.

Photo 61: front view, rotated scabbard

Photo 62: front closeup, hands

Reach between the cords and the scabbard with the left hand, take the cords from the right fingers, and withdraw the hand and cords to the left. This ties the cords around the scabbard. Adjust the cords near the butt.

Photo 63: front closeup, left hand taking cords

Photo 64: front closeup, tying cords around butt

Use the left hand to rotate the scabbard 180 degrees, edge to the left.

Photo 65: front view, rotated scabbard

Photo 66: front closeup, hands

Photo 67: front view,
left hand taking scabbard

Grasp the scabbard and cords together
with the left hand rotate the sword back
to the high horizontal position from
which you started.

Photo 68: front view, sword horizontal

Place the sword on the ground with the guard in line with your right knee, edge away from you.

Perform the seated bow.

Photo 69: front view, placing sword on floor

Photo 70: front view, *seiza,* sword on ground in front

Re-grip the sword.

Raise it to the horizontal.

Slide the left hand up to the guard, taking the familiar grip there.

Photo 71: front view, sword horizontal

Photo 72: front view, left hand on guard

Photo 73: front view, right hand removed

Release the right hand.

Photo 74: front view, *seiza*,
sword on left side ground

Place the sword on your left side,
guard in line with your knee, edge
to the outside.

Release the left hand.

If there are any other closing bows,
perform them now.

Re-grip the sword in the left hand.

Rise, right foot first, and move to the edge of the practice area.

Photo 75: front view, sword in left hand

Photo 76: left side view, standing,
sword in left hand

Transfer the sword across the front to the right hand, with the hilt to the rear and the edge downward.

Bow and leave the practice area.

Photo 77: front view, middle of pass

Photo 78: front closeup, hands

Photo 79: front view, sword in right hand

Photo 80: right side view, sword in right hand

SHOHATTO (The Initial Sword); *mae* (the front)

General Description

Sitting in seiza, *face your enemy, who is about 1.5 meters away. You sense that he is about to attack, but before he can act, you draw, striking his chest or temple. As he throws himself backward you advance and cut downward, striking his forehead. Finish the form by performing blood-cleaning and sheathing.*

Commentary

This and the three following forms are the core of sword drawing instruction. They, or ones very like them, are found in almost all systems of sword drawing as the beginning techniques. As such, they define certain general characteristics of the *Omori Ryu* style.

The forms describe in-door situations. Although the Japanese swordsman would often be outside, specifically exterior forms are not encountered until the Inner Tradition. The swordsman is in more danger when inside a house, where his movements are constrained by both the building and the social situations in which he might find himself.

This is born out by the fact that all but one of the Omori Ryu forms begin from *seiza,* the most formal sitting position. The use of this position implies that the swordsman is engaged in a formal gathering, not merely sitting alone in his house.

Japanese swordsmen would come together for formal occasions, sitting in political or social groups. Social rank and position would govern the arrangement, both within and between groups, but certain general principles would apply.

Swordsmen bonded together in some kind of group would sit close to one another and face the same direction. Their spacing would vary from only inches away to about .5 meter.

Armaments would vary, too, but follow a general rule. The less armed the swordsman is, the friendlier the gathering. If he has both swords, but the long sword is carried rather than worn in the belt, the gathering is less dangerous.

In this form, you are described as facing your opponent, who is about 1.5 meters away; too far away to be part of your group. This means that the meeting is already hostile and the enemy is known to be a threat. You should be on guard from the beginning. The fact that you're wearing your sword further indicates the hostile nature of the meeting.

Movements

Sitting in *seiza,* face the front.

To compose yourself, take three breaths.

Photo 1: front view, *seiza,* w/ sword settled

With the commencement of the third breath place both hands on the sword.

Photo 2: front view, *seiza,*
initiating horizontal draw

Photo 3: left side closeup, hands

Perform the horizontal draw, coordinating your movements with a forward right step in a kneeling posture.

The draw and step must be coordinated so that you begin the draw at the same time as you begin to rise up on both knees.

You must reach the top of the rise, and turn your toes under, at the same moment that you turn the sword a quarter turn to the left.

Without pausing, suddenly advance the right foot one step to the front. The right knee makes a right angle. The left leg stands vertically upward to the knee. The left foot stands on the toes. The lower left leg should be parallel to the right foot and clearly to the left of the center line. This is the fundamental kneeling posture of pain.

You must complete the draw, attacking the enemy's chest or temple, at the same moment your right foot comes down.

Photo 4: front view, kneeling on both knees, draw to turnover

Photo 5: left side view, kneeling on both knees, draw to turn over

Photo 6: front view, draw after turnover

Photo 7: left side view, draw after turnover

Photo 8: front view, kneeling, horizontal draw

Photo 9: left side view, kneeling, horizontal draw

Prepare for the vertical cut by swinging the sword overhead and moving the left knee forward, even with the right heel.

Photo 10: front view, kneeling, sword over left shoulder

Photo 11: left side view, kneeling, sword over left shoulder

Photo 12: front view, kneeling, *jodan*

Photo 13: left side view, kneeling, *jodan*

- Stamp the right foot down again one step forward.
- Cut downward at the center of the enemy's head.
  The sword tip stops about 15cm. from the floor.

Photo 14: front view, kneeling, downward cut

Photo 15: left side view, kneeling, downward cut

Photo 16: front view, kneeling, sword extended to right

Perform the blood-cleaning of the *Omori Ryu*.

As you swing the sword down past your face, stand half-way up on your right foot. The left knee will rise off the floor as you assume this half-standing, half-kneeling posture. This is called iai goshi *(sword drawing waist).*

Photo 17: front view, rising, sword passing face

Photo 18: front view, *iaigoshi,* end of *chiburi*

Photo 19: front view, *iaigoshi*, left foot even w/ right

In the half-sitting, half-standing posture exchange the left and right feet.

The sword is held in the right hand, away from the body on the right side, with the edge downward and the tip pointing toward the center line. It will stay in this position during the foot exchange. The left hand presses the scabbard against the left waist.

Draw the left foot up to the right. Pull the right foot back. During the time you are standing both knees will remain bent.

Photo 20: front view, *iaigoshi*, right foot pulled back

Sheath the sword.

When you turn the blade to vertical, put the right knee quietly on the floor as the action terminates.

Remain kneeling for a moment, then continue practice.

Photo 21: front view, *iaigoshi*,
scabbard turned

Photo 22: front view, sword on left hand

Photo 23: front view, *noto* to point entry

Photo 24: front view, blade inserted
to turnover

Photo 25: front view, blade after turnover

Photo 26: front view, end of *noto*

SA TO (Following Sword); *hidari* (left)

左
刀

General Description

You sit in the customary seiza *position. The enemy is on your left, about 1.5 meters away, facing the same direction as you. Before he can turn and attack, you draw, and then cut downwards, acting with the same formality as in* Shohatto.

Commentary

In this basic form you deal with an opponent who is not from a hostile group, but from one allied with your own. Your distance from your opponent means you are not part of the same group, but you are sitting on the same side, facing the same way.

Suddenly the supposed friend becomes an enemy. You, ever alert, must perceive this and respond accordingly.

Because the enemy is on the left side, you have some advantages. The enemy's sword is on the other side of his body. To use it he must turn all the way around to face you. This will slow the enemy's draw, whether horizontal or vertical.

Your weapon is on the same side as the enemy. If you can use it effectively, you should be able to strike first, provided the left step does not confuse you.

Movements

Sit with the front on your left. Look to your left and grasp the sword. Perform the horizontal draw, coordinating your movements with a leftward step in the kneeling posture.

Begin the draw at the same time as you begin to rise up on both knees.

You must reach the top of the rise, and turn your toes under, at the same movement that you turn the sword a quarter turn to the left.

Without pausing, pivot on your right knee to the left. Make sure the hilt precedes you during the pivot. You do not need to hurry the turn.

Suddenly advance the left foot one step. The left knee makes a right angle. The right leg thrusts vertically downward to the knee. The right foot stands on the toes. The lower right leg should be parallel to the left foot and clearly to the right of the center line.

You must complete the draw, attacking the enemy's chest or temple, at the same moment your left foot comes down.

Photo 1: front view, *seiza*, w/ sword settled

Photo 2: front view, *seiza*, initiating horizontal draw; looking to left

Photo 3: front view, kneeling on both knees, draw to turnover, looking to left

Photo 4: front view, draw after turnover, pivoting on right knee

Photo 5: front view, kneeling, horizontal draw, left foot forward

Photo 6: front view, kneeling, sword over left
shoulder, left foot forward

Prepare for the vertical cut by swinging the sword overhead and moving the right knee forward even with the left heel.

Photo 7: front view, kneeling, *jodan*,
left foot forward

Photo 8: front view, kneeling,
downward cut w/ left foot

- Stamp the left foot down again one step forward.

- Cut downward at the center of the enemy's head.
  In this case, the actions of the hands on the scabbard and hilt are the same as in Shohatto, *but the feet are reversed.*

Photo 9: front view, kneeling,
sword extended to right

Perform blood-cleaning.
Again the hands perform as in the
Shohatto, *but the feet are reversed.*
You will rise up on the left foot.

Photo 10: front view, rising,
sword passing face

Photo 11: front view, *iaigoshi*, end of *chiburi*

In the half-sitting, half-standing posture exchange the right and left feet.
Put the right foot forward, even with the left. Withdraw the left foot.

Photo 12: front view, *iaigoshi*,
right foot even w/ left

Photo 13: front view, *iaigoshi*,
left foot pulled back

Sheath the sword.

Kneel on the left knee. The kneel and the sheathing terminate together.

Pause and then continue your practice.

Photo 14: front view, *iaigoshi,*
scabbard turned

Photo 15: front view, sword on left hand

Photo 16: front view, *noto* to point entry

Photo 17: front view,
blade inserted to turnover

Photo 18: front view, blade after turnover

Photo 19: front view, end of *noto*

U TO (Right Sword); *migi* (right)

General Description

右

刀

You sit in the customary seiza position, with the enemy on your right, about 1.5 meters away, facing the same direction as you. Before he can turn and attack, you draw, and then cut downwards, acting with the same general formality as in Shohatto.

Commentary

This form describes a situation more dangerous than the previous ones. Here, again, you face an enemy who initially masquerades as a friend. However, because the enemy is on the right side, the advantage lies with him. In fact, you and your opponent are in exactly opposite positions as you were in the previous form, *Sa To*.

The enemy's sword is closest, now, and he can attack faster. He must step forward with his left foot, though, while you can use your right, This tends to improve your chances.

Movements

Sit with the front on your right.

Look to your right and grasp the sword.

Photo 1: front view, *seiza*, w/ sword settled

Photo 2: front view, *seiza*, initiating horizontal draw, looking to right

Perform the horizontal draw, coordinating your movements with a rightward step in the kneeling posture.

Begin the draw at the same time as you begin to rise up on both knees.

You must reach the top of the rise, and turn your toes under, at the same movement that you turn the sword a quarter turn to the left.

Without pausing, pivot on your left knee to the right. Make sure the hilt does not precede you during the pivot

Suddenly advance the right foot one step. Draw, striking the enemy's temple.

Swing the sword overhead and cut downward at the enemy from the high position.

Perform blood-cleaning as in the *Shohatto*.

Exchange the left and right feet.

Sheath the sword as before, kneeling on the right knee when about 2/3 of the blade has been sheathed.

Pause and then continue your practice.

Photo 3: front view, kneeling on both knees, draw to turnover, looking to right

Photo 4: front view, draw after turnover, pivoting on left knee

Photo 5: front view, kneeling, horizontal draw

ATARI TO (Striking Sword); *ushiro* (rear)

当

刀

General Description

You sit in the customary seiza *position. The enemy is behind you, about 1.5 meters away, facing the same direction as you. Before he can complete his attack, you turn around, face the rear, draw, and then cut downwards, acting with the same general formality as in the Sa To.*

Commentary

This is the last of the basic forms and it places you in the worst situation of the four. Here the enemy is to your rear, where he cannot be seen. When his treachery is discovered, it may be too late.

Because the distance gives the enemy the correct space he needs to attack, the first thing you must do is to turn and step closer. This takes away the enemy's advantage. As he pulls back to restore the distance, you seize control of the intermediate area to press your own attack.

You must turn 180 degrees. If you simply spin on your right knee, you risk over-balancing and missing your target. Instead, you must first open the left leg as far around to the rear as possible, step, and then snap your right leg into the correct position. This gives both distance to your step and power to your draw.

Movements

Sit facing the rear.

Look over your left shoulder and grasp the sword.

Photo 1: front view, *seiza*, w/ sword settled

Photo 2: front view, *seiza*, initiating horizontal draw, looking over left shoulder to rear

Perform the horizontal draw, coordinating your movements with a leftward-rear step in the kneeling posture.

> *Begin the draw to the front. Without pausing, pivot on your right knee to the left and rear. The left knee opens the turn. Make sure the hilt precedes you during the pivot.*
>
> *Suddenly advance the left foot one step. Draw, striking the enemy's temple.*

Swing the sword overhead and cut downward at the enemy from the high position, as in the *Sa To.*

Perform blood-cleaning as in *Sa To.*

Exchange the right and left feet.

Perform the *Sa To* substitution step, sheath the sword, and terminate the sheathing by kneeling.

Pause and then continue your practice.

Photo 3: front view, kneeling on both knees, draw to turnover, looking to rear over left shoulder

Photo 4: front view, kneeling, draw after turnover, left foot forward

Photo 5: front view, kneeling, horizontal draw, left foot forward

INYO SHINTAI (Advancing-Retreating Movement); *yae gaki* (doubled fences)

General Description

You sit in the customary seiza *position, faced by two enemies, sitting one behind the other, at about 1.5 and 3 meters. You draw before the first can attack, but he is only wounded and begins to retreat. You pursue by standing up and cutting downward. You then perform a new blood-cleaning and sheath your sword.*

The second enemy stands and attacks you with a downward cut. Withdraw one step and draw at his waist. Then advance and cut downwards. The form ends with the usual blood-cleaning and sheathing.

Commentary

There are two enemies in this form and they are both openly hostile. They are sitting in rows, and can attack you sequentially. The closer one presents the immediate threat, since he will attack first, but it is the second one who is more dangerous.

The first enemy is close enough to attack while kneeling, with either a horizontal or vertical draw. You have seen this before, in *Shohatto*. You respond in essentially the same way, and win.

The second enemy, however, has both the time and space to stand and press his attack with a strong downward cut. The power of a standing cut is greater than one done from kneeling. His footwork can be more complicated and more responsive to your defenses.

Even while your are dealing with the first opponent, you must react to the second. Your choice of the smaller, quicker Eishin Ryu blood-cleaning shows that you do not want to open yourself as widely as an Omori Ryu blood-cleaning would. Similarly, the careful sheathing demonstrates your watchfulness.

You aren't sure that the second opponent will attack, and you are willing to disengage. This is demonstrated by your returning to a kneeling position during blood-cleaning.

When the second enemy attacks, you pull back one large step to dodge his cut and counterattack. When the enemy falls, you follow him down to finish the action.

Movements

Sit facing the front.

Draw at the first enemy, essentially the same as in the *Shohatto*.
The enemy is assumed to be only wounded by this draw and is able to withdraw to the rear.

Photo 1: front view, *seiza*, w/ sword settled

Photo 2: front view, kneeling,
horizontal draw

Without delay, swing the sword overhead and stand.
Take most of your weight on the right foot.

Photo 3: front view, rising,
sword over left shoulder

Photo 4: left side view, rising,
sword over left shoulder

Photo 5: front view, standing, *jodan*

- Advance the left foot one step.

- Cut downwards at the enemy from the high position.
  Having cut down, the sword will be at or a little below horizontal.

Photo 6: front view, standing, downward cut, left foot forward

Photo 7: left side view, standing cut, left foot forward

Detach the left hand from the hilt and place it over the scabbard at the waist.

Photo 8: front view, standing, left hand on scabbard at waist

Photo 9: front closeup, left hand

Photo 10: front view, end of *eishin chiburi*

Perform blood-cleaning by opening the sword to the right side.

At the end of blood-cleaning, the hilt slants to the right. The sword point remains on the front center line. The blade slants downward, edge to the front, to the degree of the previously described running water. This is called the blood-cleaning of the Eishin Ryu, or suihei osame to "swihei osame to" (the horizontal stopping sword).

Kneel on the right knee.

Photo 11: front view, squatting, end of *noto*

Sheath the sword from this position, but just before the finish, draw back the left foot and lower the body until the heel touches the buttocks.

Sheath almost to the sword guard, but leave a little blade showing. It is important that you be aware of the danger of the second enemy. Demonstrate remaining heart throughout.

Photo 12: front view, rising, draw to turnover

Because the second enemy attacks from the front, withdraw the left foot well to the rear.

Lift the right knee from the floor, rise on the balls of both feet and step backwards with the left foot.

Photo 13: left side view, left foot pulled back

- Stand and draw at the enemy's waist.

  The backward left step gives you the space you need to dodge the enemy's overhead cut. Your draw can be accomplished either by standing with the right foot forward, or by immediately kneeling on the left knee, in a very quick bobbing action. This last is considered more advanced.

Photo 14: front view, horizontal draw

Photo 15: left side view, horizontal draw

- Swing the sword overhead and kneel on the left knee.
- Move the left knee forward as far as the right heel.

Photo 16: front view, kneeling,
sword over left shoulder

Photo 17: left side view, kneeling,
sword over left shoulder

Photo 18: front view, kneeling, *jodan*

Photo 19: left side view, kneeling, *jodan*

- Advance the right foot one step.

- Cut downward at the enemy essentially as in the *Shohatto*.

Perform the blood-cleaning of the *Omori Ryu*.

Perform the substitution step, sheath the sword and terminate the sheathing by kneeling.

Pause and continue your practice.

RYU TO (Flowing Sword); *ukenagashi* (parrying)

General Description

流

刀

Sitting customarily, you find your enemy 1.5 meters away on the left side, facing the same direction as you. He suddenly stands and attacks you from the left with an overhead downward cut.

Deflect the enemy's sword with your own while dodging to the right front. The moment the enemy's sword falls through the deflection, cut at his left waist, at the scabbard. The form ends with a new sheathing method.

Commentary

Again, a supposed friend has become an enemy. This is a common theme in the forms.

The enemy rises from sitting, drawing his sword vertically, and makes a strong downward cut at your head. All this will take some time, time in which you have to react.

Japanese sword drawing uses few defensive techniques. The overhead parry, used in this form, is the most common. When contrasted with European fencing, the scarcity of defense seems a surprising lack. In fact, it follows from the spirit of sword drawing and the swordsman's code of conduct.

The Japanese swordsman's emphasis is on victory, not defense. A proverb says that if the enemy cuts his skin, the swordsman will cut the enemy's bones. Hence, the delivery of an effective attack is paramount. If it costs the swordsman his life to win, it is worth it.

Japanese fencing does, of course, contain many parrying techniques, and sometimes these appear in sword drawing forms. However, the main action is to counterattack, not to defend. To this end the swordsman relies on his speed, power, and intuition.

This form, Ryu To, describes what happens when a defense is used. Your immediate reaction is to protect your head and shoulder. You step forward to move your head out of the line of attack and draw your sword to intercept his cut. You must catch the enemy's blade on your sword blade ridge, not your edge. The edge is too brittle and may chip. You must catch his sword within 15 cm of your sword guard. Any farther than this and you cannot withstand the impact.

Even so, the shock will be jarring. Your right elbow is slightly bent to help absorb some of it, but a two-handed cut is intrinsically stronger than a single-handed parry. His blade will force yours down. This is not a test of wills, but the result of unequal forces. It will happen in a flash, which is why the first steps of the form must be very quick.

You deliberately give way, standing up while his sword is pushing your point down. As his blade slides off yours, and before he can recover, you counter-attack.

Movements

Photo 1: front view, *seiza*, sword settled

Sit with the front on your left.

Suddenly the enemy stands, draws, steps forward and cuts at your head.

Photo 2: front view, kneeling, vertical draw to release, left foot forward

Photo 3: front view, kneeling, deflection

- Turn your face toward the enemy.
- Advance the left foot one step to the right front.
- Grasp the hilt with your right fingers on the side and quickly draw the sword high over the front of the left shoulder.
- Deflect the enemy's sword with the blade ridge of your own, at about 20cm. from the sword guard.
  This is a vertical draw, which covers the shoulder while you dodge the cut.
  At the moment of impact, the right elbow should be relaxed a little.

- Without delay stand up by advancing the right foot diagonally to the right front, at about a 45-degree angle.

- Continue the deflection as you rise by drawing your right elbow down to your right side and your right fist to the top of your right shoulder, bringing the sword clearly horizontal behind your neck.
  Shift your weight onto the right foot.
    The movement of your body will displace the enemy's sword.

- As the enemy's sword slides through the deflection, point the left foot at the enemy.

Photo 4: front view, rising,
right foot forward

Photo 5: front view, standing,
sword behind neck, left foot pointing

- Bring the right heel to the left heel.

- Taking hold of the hilt with the left hand, cut at the enemy's left waist, targeting at the scabbard.
  The toes point a little to the left of the line joining you.
    The tips of both feet unfold like a fan, making angle about 90 degrees. Both knees should be bent. The rhythm of the left-right steps should be irregular (x-xx).
    The blade cuts downward at a 45-degree angle. This is sometimes called the kesagiri *(priest's stole cut).*

Photo 6: front view, standing, heels together, both hands on hilt

Photo 7: front view, standing, strike at enemy's scabbard

Photo 8: front view, *gedan*

- While in the posture of the strike, change the direction of the feet, turning right to the front.

- Move the sword to the middle position.

- Pull the left foot to the rear.

- Drop the sword point to the low position, about 15cm. above the floor.

Photo 9: front view, standing, sword drawn towards left

Draw the hilt upward and to the left so that the left fingers point downwards and the right point upward, and the sword point stops about 10cm. from the right knee.

At this point both hands are a little relaxed. The left elbow approaches the height of the shoulders.

Reverse the grip of the right hand on the hilt.

Photo 10: front view, standing,
reverse right hand grip

Photo 11: front close up, right hand

Photo 12: front view, standing,
left hand on scabbard

Remove the left hand from the hilt
and grasp the mouth of the scabbard.

Holding the sword in the reversed right
hand, roll it over by the left elbow so that
the right palm faces upward and the
sword points to the left.
  *Rest the reversed sword on the left hand
  at the scabbard mouth.*

Photo 13: front view, standing,
sword halfway through swing

Photo 14: front view, standing,
sword on left hand

Draw the sword to the right with the right hand in one stroke, and sheath the blade.

When the blade in 2/3 inserted, kneel on the left knee.

As usual the kneeling and the sheathing terminate together. During the first part of the sheathing the right hand inserts the blade horizontally; as the sheathing finishes the sword rotates to the vertical, edge up. This form of sheathing is called the yakuza no osame ho *(gambler's sheathing style), and is not much used.*

Photo 15: front view, standing, sword drawn to right

Photo 16: front closeup, point entry

Photo 17: front view, kneeling, end of *noto*

At the end of sheathing slide the right hand forward and momentarily cover the pommel.

JUN TO (Obedient Sword); *kaishaku* (assistant at suicide)

General Description

順

刀

In this form you perform the movements of the assistant at seppuku *(Japanese ritual suicide). This form differs from the rest because, instead of an enemy, you now face a friend.*

Sit in seiza, *facing the front. You are to the left side and about 50 cm to 60 cm to the rear of your person, who will be facing to your left. Watch for the suitable moment, then draw your sword and rise. Your person will use a dagger, or short sword, to commit suicide. This will be placed on a small offering stand in front of him. As he leans forward to take the dagger, you will cut downward at the back of his neck. The form then finishes with the same sheathing as in* Ryu To.

Commentary

The Japanese developed the concept of ritual suicide early. It originated on the battlefield, to prevent an enemy from killing a swordsman and confiscating his property, family, or social position. Gradually, it spread to other situations until it became a method to avoid disgrace of any sort.

For men, suicide is done by slicing the abdomen in a prescribed pattern: horizontally from left to right, continuing vertically up the right side, then vertically down the left side, making an open-sided triangle. Needless to say, most people did not complete the cut before being overcome by pain and shock.

To prevent any unsightly behavior, the person committing suicide was accompanied by a second. His function is to kill his friend when he shows any signs of weakening. He does this with a special cut that leaves the head intact. The cut, when done correctly, only severs the spinal chord between the fifth and sixth cervical vertebrae.

In more recent times, before suicide was outlawed, it was often used as a form of execution. As the practice degenerated, the victim was often not even given a knife, but instead, a fan was placed on the offering stand in its place. When the victim bent forward to reach for the fan, his second struck, killing him instantly.

Since a swordsman's suicide took place before a large group of his peers, the actions are performed very formally. It is important not to depart from the spirit of the form and to regard the action as a mere "killing."

Movements

Photo 1: front view, *seiza,* w/ sword settled

Sit facing the front.

Photo 2: front view, partially drawn,
on left knee, looking to the left

- Fix your eyes on the front (your person).
- Quietly turn 90-degrees to the right on the left knee.
- Quietly advance the right foot one large step.
- Draw the sword, blade up, toward the right knee until about 1/3 is drawn.

Photo 3: front view, standing,
point emerging

- With your eyes still fixed on your person, stand up.
- Draw the sword upward, edge still up. *The sword point leaves the scabbard the instant you fully stand.*

- Point the left foot at your person.

- Draw the right foot over to the left.

- Slide the left hand down the scabbard and press it, palm open, against the scabbard at the waist.

- Rotate the sword vertically past the face, turning your right hand at the end so that the sword is carried over the right shoulder.
  The heels are together; the toes are fanned out. Stand erect with the knees slightly bent.

  The right hand is in front of the shoulder at about chest height. The sword angles back, as if carried on the shoulder, but clearly not touching it. You must maintain this posture without moving.

Photo 4: front view, feet together,
sword passing the face

Photo 5: front view, sword over shoulder

Photo 6: front view, feet together, *jodan*

- Match your breathing to that of your person.

- Raise the sword to the high position, holding it in both hands.
  Because your intention is to aid your person, you must watch closely, gathering your concentration.

  The sword approaches the high position directly from the right shoulder.

Photo 7: front view, standing,
downward cut

- At the proper moment quietly advance the right foot one step.

- Just as you step down on the right foot, cut at the back of your person's neck. *Strike at about a 30 to 40 degree angle. You must control the cut so that you do not cut through the skin or muscles of his throat; cut only through the spinal chord. Do not let his head drop. The blade must stop at the horizontal the moment you strike at the neck. You must train to finish your strike clearly as the right foot touches.*

Quietly pull back from the neck.
 Pull back about 20cm.

Move the sword to the middle position.

From this posture, perform the same sheathing as in the Flowing Sword.

Pause and continue your practice.

GYAKU TO (Reversed Sword); *tsukekomi* (taking advantage)

General Description

逆

刀

While sitting, you are attacked from the front by a standing enemy who crowds in with a downward cut. You fall back one step while parrying to the left.

Recovering immediately, you strike at the enemy, who flees to the rear. You press your attack, cornering him. The form ends with a new blood-cleaning and a new sheathing.

Commentary

The enemy is already standing. He catches you by surprise, rushing at you to deliver his cut. This is quite different than Ryu To, where the enemy had to stand and draw before attacking. You have much less to react and little time for an effective parry.

Instead of relying on the parry for protection, you employ a more basic technique: you dodge. You begin the form as if you have time to draw and parry, but quickly see this is impossible. The force of the enemy's attack is like a solid wall. You cannot draw your sword any farther forward. Instead, you pull backwards, away from your hilt and the sword draws itself.

This backward step pulls your head out of the target area. If it is done correctly, your enemy will miss, overshooting his mark, and will be open for a counter attack.

Just to be sure, you raise the sword to the parrying position. Ideally, the enemy's sword misses yours completely. If not, you must be prepared for the shock.

Receive his blade on your sword blade ridge as close to the guard as possible. The right elbow takes some of the force; the rest must be dissipated downward over your left shoulder.

In any case, you counterattack immediately, striking the opponent twice. Then you withdraw to study the situation. Finding that more action is required, you strike the enemy a third time. Although this seems sufficient, some instructors add a thrust to the form, done just before the final blood-cleaning.

Movements

Photo 1: front view, *seiza*, sword settled

Sit facing the front.

Photo 2: front view, on left knee,
sword drawn to right knee

- Respond to the enemy's attack by advancing the right foot a half step to the front.

- Raise the hips, standing up on the left tiptoes.

- Draw the sword about 15cm to 20cm. *The sword is drawn to the right knee.*

Photo 3: front view, standing,
point emerging

- Since the enemy is already crowding his attack too close, stand up, drawing the right foot back to the left.

- Draw the sword upward to the right.

- Parry the enemy's sword to the left, protecting the head and left shoulder.
  Because the enemy can adjust his attack, it is desirable to move the left foot back a small step before the right foot moves to it.

  The handguard must not move any further forward than the right knee. You should feel as if a wall prevents this and that the sword can be drawn only because you step backwards. The sword point comes out just as the right foot comes back to the left.

  The right hand extends to the upper right, the right elbow is stretched out, but relaxed. Although the parry is important, the main point is to adjust the interval to your advantage, so that the enemy's attack misses.

Photo 4: front view, standing,
feet together, parry

Photo 5: left side view, parry

Photo 6: front view, *jodan*

- Immediately turn the sword out of the parry to the high position, adding the left hand.

Photo 7: front view, standing, downward cut

- Advance the right foot one step.
- Cut downward at the enemy about as far as his jaw line.
  Cut downward the instant the left hand grasps the hilt.

Photo 8: front view, left *jodan*

- Because the enemy is only slightly wounded and retreats, advance the left foot a large step.
- Raise the sword to the high position.

Photo 9: front view, standing, low downward cut

- Advance the right foot a large step.
- Cut downward at the enemy to the vicinity of the navel.

- Move the left foot up to the right and pull the right foot to the rear.
- Raise the sword to the high position.
  During the raising, demonstrate remaining heart.

Photo 10: front view, feet together, sword at *chudan*

Photo 11: front view, left *jodan*

Photo 12: front view, kneeling on right knee, downward cut

- Without warning, drop the right knee to the floor.
- Cut down on the enemy, feeling as if you are dropping a great weight.

Detach the right hand from the hilt and re-grip with the hand reversed.

Photo 13: front view, kneeling, reversed right hand

Photo 14: right side closeup closeup, hands

- Detach the left hand from the hilt and rotate the blade to edge up.
- Supporting the back of the blade with the base of the left index finger, palm up, pull the right hand up to the right shoulder, gently withdrawing the sword about 30cm through the left fingers.
  This is called chi nugui *"chi nugwi" (blood-wiping).*

Photo 15: front view, sword on left hand

Photo 16: front closeup, hands

Photo 17: front view, kneeling,
end of *chi nugui*

Photo 18: front view, kneeling, blade flat, left hand on scabbard

- Remain kneeling, with the right hand reversed, move the sword to the outside, with the blade flat, in one stroke.

- Grasp the scabbard mouth with the left hand.

Photo 19: front view, kneeling, point entry

- Drawing the sword out in a straight line, place the point in the scabbard.

- Sheath the sword

- Pull back the left foot to the right heel

Stand up, stepping to the front with the left foot.

Bring the right foot up to the left, pause and continue your practice.

SEICHU TO (Center Strengthened Sword); *tsukikage* (moonlight)

General Description

勢
中
刀

Your enemy comes from your right side, attacking with a standing overhead cut. Drawing while rising from the sitting position, you cut at the enemy's forearms. While the enemy retreats from this attack, you follow, cutting downward at his forehead. You then finish the form by performing the Omori Ryu *blood-cleaning and sheathing.*

Commentary

Again, a standing enemy attacks. In this form you do not even attempt a defense, but leap immediately to the offensive.

The draw begins as a vertical one, but aimed toward the opponent on the right.

Simultaneously, you rise to the half-standing, half-kneeling posture characteristic of Japanese sword drawing. The rise requires that you be strongly centered and that your motions be absolutely correct.

Two sets of movements must occur simultaneously, uniting the upper and lower body. The lower body must direct and position the legs; the upper body, the sword. Paradoxically, the upper body movements are responsible for your rise.

Upon rising to you knees you must immediately advance to right kneeling posture. You must swing the left lower leg 90-degrees to the right until it faces the enemy, and simultaneously raise the right leg one step forward. Your feet move directly to their positions from *seiza*. This action will turn the upper body so that you will be facing the enemy directly, in the position to make the strike.

The other motion is the draw itself. Draw the scabbard across your stomach and begin a vertical draw. It actually slides across the chest, while you turn beside it to put it into the usual position at your left side.

Just as your feet come into position, the sword point leaves the scabbard and you stand up to make the strike. Do not stand by the strength of your legs alone, but feel as if the sword pulls you up on its way to the target.

This form is said to be called moonlight, not because it was elegant, but because the draw resembles the moon's last quarter.

Movements

Sit with the front on your right.

Photo 1: front view, *seiza*, w/ sword settled

- When the enemy attacks with an overhead cut rotate on the left knee 90-degrees to the right.

- While turning rise to a half-sitting, half-standing posture by advancing the right foot one step toward the enemy.

- Draw the sword upward to the right about 45-degrees and cut at the enemy's forearms.
  The tip of the left foot, and the right knee face the enemy.
    Do not stamp.
    Feel as though the cut carries through both forearms. The draw cannot be performed properly without the correct body posture. The hip action must be strong and definite.

Photo 2: front view, on left knee,
vertical draw

Photo 3: left side view, on left knee,
vertical draw

Photo 4: front view, *iaigoshi,* forearm cut

Photo 5: front view, feet together,
parry over left shoulder

- As the enemy retreats, follow by advancing the left foot up to the right.

- Swing the sword overhead by parrying over the left shoulder.

- Just as the sword comes into the high position, add the left hand to the hilt.

Photo 6: front view, feet together, *jodan*

Photo 7: front view, standing, downward cut

- Advance again by stepping forward with the right foot.

- Cut downward at the center of the enemy's forehead.
  The sword strikes the enemy's forehead the same moment the right foot touches the ground. From the draw to the strike the movements are done in quick succession.

From the position at the end of the cut, perform the blood-cleaning of the *Omori Ryu.*

Exchange your feet.

Sheath your sword as in *Shohatto,* kneeling at the end.

Raise the right knee, stand up and move the left foot up even with the right.

Pause and continue your practice.

KORAN TO (Tiger Fighting Sword); *oikaze* (pursuing wind)

General Description

While walking, you are confronted with an enemy. Before he can attack, you quickly draw, attacking his chest or head. As he flees to the rear, you pursue and cut him down. The form ends with the usual Omori Ryu *blood-cleaning and sheathing.*

Commentary

This is the only standing form in the *Omori Ryu.* It is not specifically situated out-doors, but the amount of distance you travel make that a likely possibility.

Standing with you feet together, you walk toward the front, beginning with the left foot. You step left-right-left in a casual manner. During the second left step you become aware that an enemy is about to attack, and begin the action of the form.

The manner in which you change from casual walking to a sudden attack is like the spring of a tiger. Hence, the name of the form.

This form is significant in that it is the only one performed entirely standing. There is no kneel after the sheathing.

Movements

Stand facing the front.

Begin walking to the front with the left foot.

When the left foot steps forward a second time grasp the hilt with the right hand and the scabbard with the left.

> *Point the tip of the left foot to the front. The moment the left foot advances begin the draw.*

Photo 1: front view, standing, sword settled

Photo 2: front view, left foot forward, initiating horizontal draw

Photo 3: front view, standing,
large horizontal draw

- Advance the right foot a large step.
- Draw the sword essentially as in the *Shohatto*.

  You should attack as suddenly as a tiger attacks its prey. This may be why the form is named Tiger Fighting. Your response to the enemy's attack should be immediate. Your draw should slice the air.

Photo 4: front view, left *jodan*

- Advance the left foot one step to the front.
- Swing the sword overhead by parrying over the left shoulder.

- Immediately advance the right foot a large step.
- Strike down the enemy.

  You must clearly pursue the enemy. Observers should be able to discern the enemy's actions from your own.

  The distinctive feature of this form is the sudden difference in the quality between this pursuit and the initial walking.

Photo 5: front view, standing, downward cut

Having cut down, perform the *Omori Ryu* blood-cleaning.

Move the left foot forward to the right.

Pull the right foot back half a step and sheath the sword.

Do not finish sheathing by kneeling.

Pause and continue your practice.

NUKI UCHI (Sudden Attack)

General Description

抜
打

You are sitting face to face with an enemy who is much closer than before, about 75cm. Before he can attack, you swiftly draw your sword. The space between you is too narrow to permit this draw to be an attack, so you immediate swing the sword overhead and cut downward at the enemy's forehead. The form finishes with the blood-cleaning of the Eishin Ryu, *as in* Inyo Shintai, *and then sheathing.*

Commentary

A swordsman would sit as close to an enemy as is done in this form only if he thought himself safe. The fact that this proves not to be the case reinforces a growing perception of the world of the Japanese swordsman, with its insecure political and social relationships.

A horizontal draw requires a minimum distance to be effective. From kneeling, a horizontal draw extends about 1.5 meters from your original sitting position. This is why the beginning forms of this Tradition placed the opponent at this distance. Other distances will be introduced in later Traditions.

One way to decrease the effective distance of the draw is to take a shorter forward step. Because the enemy in this form is so close, you cannot take any steps at all.

The form must be done without pause, uniting the movements in an unbroken sequence. It also must be done without regard to pain, as the knees are lifted from and slammed back to the floor.

Movements

Sit facing the front.

Photo 1: front view, *seiza,* sword settled

Photo 2: front view, kneeling on both knees, sword drawn to right

- Grasp the hilt with your right hand and the scabbard with your left.

- Raise the hips, standing up the tiptoes of both feet.

- At the same time, suddenly draw the sword to the diagonal right front, blade facing upward.

- Spread your knees.

Photo 3: front view, kneeling on both knees, sword horizontal

- As soon as the sword point separates from the scabbard, swing the sword overhead by clearly swinging it around the outside of the left elbow, adding the left hand as it comes into the high position.

- Clap your knees together.
  At the moment of separation the blade will pass through a position in which the blade will be horizontal, edge up.

  You must push yourself up as the sword comes to the high position. Your knees should leave the ground and slap together while you are in the air.

Photo 4: front view, knees in air, *jodan*

Photo 5: front closeup, knees

Photo 6: front view, kneeling
on both knees, downward cut

- From the high position cut downward at the enemy's forehead.

- Suddenly spread your knees again as they return to the floor.
  Your knees must make a knocking sound as they strike the floor. Having cut down, both heels will be close together.

In this position perform the blood-cleaning of the *Eishin Ryu,* as in the *Inyo Shintai.*

Sheath the sword while you lower your buttocks onto your heels.
   This occurs the moment the sheathing is finished.

Quietly bring the knees together, even in front.

Advance the right foot one step to the front, stand up and bring the left foot up even with the right.

Pause and continue your practice.

INYO SHINTAI KAEWAZA (Advancing-Retreating Movement, Alternate Technique)

General Description

陰
陽
進
退
替
業

As indicated by its name, this form presents an alternate set of movements for the rationale of Inyo Shintai.

As in Inyo Shintai, *you have two enemies. You deal with the first as before. The second enemy then attacks, but this time cuts at your right leg. You withdraw, beating away his attack with your sword, and then counter-attack with a downward cut. The form ends with the blood-cleaning and sheathing of the* Omori Ryu.

Commentary

The commentary on Inyo Shintai applies to this form as well. You must be aware of the danger of the second opponent as you deal with the first, but you also must not provoke him.

The second opponent stands and attacks you, as in Inyo Shintai, but is quicker than in that form. He presses his attack against a different target, too. Where before he cut downward at your head, here he cuts diagonally at your right leg.

Because he is faster, you must defend your leg before you can counterattack. You do this by employing another defensive technique, the *harai* (the beat). This is not a simple deflection, in which his sword slides off, but an aggressive strike to the side of his blade by your own.

When you draw your sword the second time to beat away your enemy's strike, you must adjust your grip on the hilt. Normally in the horizontal draw, the thumb is placed under the hilt and later rotated to the side; in the vertical draw, the thumb is rotated to the side from the beginning. In the second draw in this form you do not place the thumb underneath at all, but grip the hilt from the top with the thumb on the side. If you try to execute the beat with any other grip you'll see why.

The beat is not so much a sideways motion as a diagonal one. The sword is drawn to the front. When it comes free of the scabbard it is immediately reversed and pulled backwards in the beat. Your blade strikes his with a glancing, but hard blow. If your beat has been ineffective and his sword continues on its arc to strike your leg, your blade will still be in between, protecting you.

When you swing the sword into the high position you must use the left hand to support the sword while you shift the right hand around to the normal grip.

This form was not originally part of the Omori Ryu, but was added later.

Movements

Photo 1: front view, squatting, end of *noto*

From sitting, confront the first enemy with the movements of the *Inyo Shintai* form, up to the first sheathing.
Insert the blade up to the collar.

- Since the second enemy advances, attacking your right leg, shift your grip on the hilt to the top.
- Draw the sword, edge up.

Photo 2: right side closeup, hilt

Photo 3: front view, standing,
draw until point emerges

Photo 4: front view, standing,
halfway through *harai*

- Stand and pull the left foot
  one large step backward.

- The moment the sword point clears
  the scabbard, turn the hilt to the rear,
  swinging the sword sharply around
  your right hip so that it now points forward, edge up, point down, clearly preserving your right leg by beating away
  the enemy's sword.
  *The position of the beat the sword
  is parallel to the right foot. The movements of the beat must express more
  than merely receiving the enemy's
  sword. You must feel as though your
  sword moves straight to the beat like
  an arrow.*

Photo 5: front view, standing, *harai*

Photo 6: right side view, *harai*

Photo 7: front view, standing,
sword moving to *jodan*

- Suddenly move the left knee forward to the right heel.

- Swing the sword overhead.

- Cut downward at the enemy.
  You will be in a kneeling position.

Photo 8: front view, kneeling, *jodan*

Photo 9: front view, kneeling, downward cut

Perform the same blood-cleaning as in the *Shohatto*.

Perform the same sheathing as in the *Shohatto*.

Pause and continue your practice.

4. The Middle Tradition: Eishin Ryu

BACKGROUND

The *Hasegawa Eishin Ryu* (Deep River Valley Excellent Faith System) is another style of sword drawing. It is often simply referred to as the *Eishin Ryu* (Excellent Faith System). The *Eishin Ryu* is currently taught as the Middle Tradition of the *Muso Shinden Ryu*, following the study of the *Omori Ryu*. As such, it is regarded as more difficult than the *Omori Ryu*.

It contains ten forms. All but the last begin from *tate hiza* (the drawn-up knee sitting position). This position is more difficult than the formal sitting position.

The drawn-up knee position is said to be an older sitting position and to derive from the sitting method used when wearing Japanese armor, in which the shin guards prevented formal sitting.

Like the *Omori Ryu*, the basic actions of any *Eishin Ryu* form belong to the four standard classes: drawing, cutting, blood- cleaning, and sheathing.

The forms are designated by name, as follows:

> *Yokogumo* (Bank of Clouds)
>
> *Tora Issoku* (Pair of Tigers)
>
> *Inazuma* (Lightning)
>
> *Ukigumo* (Floating Clouds)
>
> *Yamaoroshi* (Mountain Wind)
>
> *Iwanami* (Waves Breaking Against Rocks)
>
> *Urokogaeshi* (Returning Pattern)
>
> *Namigaeshi* (Returning Waves)
>
> *Taki Otoshi* (Dropping Waterfall)
>
> *Nuki Uchi* (Sudden Attack)

In the descriptions that follow, the forms will have the structure introduced in the previous chapter. The other usual conventions of the descriptions will still be followed.

DISTINCTIVE FEATURES

As noted previously, the first nine forms begin in the drawn-up knee position. The movements from this position are more varied than in the *Omori Ryu*.

In the First Tradition the forms used a single-step forwards to define the drawing interval, *maai* (the distance needed to reach the enemy with the sword). The Middle Tradition often defines the drawing interval with a single-step backwards. This is because the enemy is assumed to be sitting much closer than previously. Frequently, he is assumed to be sitting immediately adjacent.

The cutting actions that follow the draw often involve more complex steps than previously.

The blood-cleaning of the Middle Tradition is quite different from that of the First. It involves much less sword movement. Care must be taken that it is still conducted to demonstrate remaining heart.

Photo 1: front view, kneeling,
end of overhead cut

While in a kneeling posture the left hand releases the hilt and grips the scabbard at the left hip. The right hand, retaining its grasp, opens to the right, ending with a slight snap as the elbow straightens. The sword assumes a slight downward diagonal position. The reader has already encountered this in the first part of the *Inyo Shintai* form of the *Omori Ryu*.

Photo 2: front view, kneeling,
left hand on scabbard at waist

Photo 3: front view, kneeling,
sword moving to right

Photo 4: front view, kneeling,
end of *eishin chiburi*

The sheathing is also new.

In the First Tradition the back of the blade was placed at the scabbard mouth in the vicinity of the hand guard. In the Middle Tradition, the back of the blade is placed at the scabbard mouth in the vicinity of the center of the blade.

As before, the sword is sheathed by pulling it to the right in a single movement, until the point slips into the scabbard, and then inserting slowly. Because the sword is started closer to the point, the sheathing is faster. The last third of the sheathing, as before, is done with deliberate slowness to demonstrate remaining heart.

Photo 5: front view, kneeling,
blade on left hand

Photo 6: left side closeup, left hand

Photo 7: front view, kneeling, point entry

Photo 8: front view, kneeling,
noto after point entry

Photo 9: front view, squatting,
end of *eishin noto*

PRELIMINARY EXERCISES

Because the initial posture of all but one of the forms in the *Eishin Ryu* is that of the drawn-up knee, the obvious preliminary exercise involves assuming that position.

Sitting in *Tate Hiza*

The sword is inserted into the belt with the standard formalities, while sitting formally.

The Middle Tradition may be practiced directly, or may follow a period of practice of the First Tradition.

Photo 10: front view, standing, sword settled

- With the sword already inserted in the belt, advance to the place of practice.

- Hold the sword with the left hand, thumb on the guard.

Carry the left foot one step backward.
The left foot should be in line with the right.

Photo 11: front view, kneeling,
left hand on sword

- Slowly settle into a left kneeling posture.

- Allow the left toes to straighten and lie on the floor.

- Sit down directly over the top of the left heel.

- To avoid tangling the right foot in the right wide trouser leg, sweep away the inside of the cuff to the right with the right hand.

- Pull the right foot back toward the left ankle and then position the heel against the lower left leg behind the knee.
  The outside right instep rests on the floor. The right toes point clearly away from the left knee, toward the front. The right knee is not allowed to touch the floor, being raised 10 cm to 20 cm. Take care that the scabbard does not strike the floor.

Rest the hands on the thighs, palms up.
Both elbows bend slightly.

Photo 12: front view, kneeling,
sweep away cuff

Photo 13: front view, *tate hiza*

Photo 14: front view, *tate hiza*

Rising from *Tate Hiza*

- Grip the scabbard with the left hand, thumb over the guard.

- Roll the right knee to the vertical.

Photo 15: front view, right knee vertical

Photo 16: front view, kneeling,
left hand on sword

Rise to a left kneeling position.

Photo 17: front view, standing, sword settled

Advance the right foot slightly and stand up.

YOKOGUMO (Bank of Clouds)

General Description

This form is closely related to Shohatto *in the First Tradition. Sit facing your enemy, and draw, striking his temple. Follow this with a center cut to the head. Then finish the form with blood-cleaning and sheathing.*

Commentary

As in *Shohatto*, you respond to your enemy with a horizontal draw followed by a downward cut. However, everything else about *Yokogumo* is different.

Rising from *tate hiza* is quite different than from *seiza*. In *seiza*, the weight is initially taken on both knees equally and then shifted to the supporting knee. In *tate hiza*, the weight is initially on the left foot, then shifted to the left knee, and finally to the right foot. This allows the left foot to be pulled back much more easily than in *seiza*.

At the end of the draw you will be half-standing, half-kneeling in the typical sword drawing posture. You will return the left knee to the floor while swinging the sword into the high position and strike the enemy when you are kneeling.

Movements

Photo 1: front view, *tate hiza*

Sit in the drawn-up knee position, facing the front.

Photo 2: front view, *tate hiza*, initiating horizontal draw

Photo 3: front view, *tate hiza*, right knee vertical

Photo 4: front view, *iaigoshi*, horizontal draw

- Sensing your enemy's intentions, grip the sword with both hands, right on the hilt and left on the scabbard, and begin to draw the sword, edge up.

- Raise the right knee toward vertical.

- Taking weight on the right foot, pull the left foot back one step.

- Strike the enemy's temple.
  Rotate the right knee into the space freed by the drawing right arm. Lift the left kneecap high off the floor, but keep the hips low. You will finish in the half-sitting half-standing posture typical of sword drawing.

Photo 5: front view, *iaigoshi*,
sword over left shoulder

- Having drawn the sword, swing the sword overhead.

- Move the left knee forward and kneel by the right heel.

- Pull the scabbard back into position.

Photo 6: front view, kneeling, *jodan*

Photo 7: front view, kneeling, downward cut

- Advance the right foot.

- Cut downward at the enemy.

Perform the *Eishin Ryu* blood-cleaning.

Sheath the sword in the manner of the *Eishin Ryu*.

When the sword is approximately one-third sheathed, while expressing remaining heart, quietly pull the right foot back to the left. The form ends with sheathing, when the heels are about 15 cm. apart. The buttocks rest lightly on the tops of the heels.

TORA ISSOKU (Pair of Tigers)

General Description

The enemy, seated in front of you, attacks your right foot. As in the twelfth form of the First Tradition, the Inyo Shintai Kaewaza, *you first stop the enemy's sword. Making use of the enemy's retreat, you cut him down from the high position.*

Commentary

This form uses the beat to block the enemy's strike. That means that you must grip the hilt from the top with the thumb extended down the side. The sword is drawn to the front, then quickly reversed to the beat, cleanly striking the side of the enemy's blade.

At the moment of the beat you will be in the typical half-standing, half-kneeling posture. From here you will kneel while swinging the sword into the high position. You must use the left hand to support the sword while you shift the right hand around to the normal grip.

Movements

Sit facing the front in the drawn-up knee position.

Photo 1: front view, *tate hiza*

Photo 2: front view, *tate hiza,*
initiating horizontal draw

- As the enemy cuts at your right foot, grasp the hilt and scabbard.

- Raise the right knee toward vertical.

- Pull the left foot one step backwards.

- Gripping from the top, swiftly draw the sword.
  The blade remains vertical.

Photo 3: front view, *tate hiza,*
right knee vertical

Photo 4: front view, standing,
draw til point emerges

Clearly preserving your right leg, ward off the enemy's sword with your sword blade ridge.

At this moment, your hips twist a little to the left. During the draw, when the sword point is within 9cm. of being free, the sword springs cleanly to the block. The blade is edge up, point to the front.

Photo 5: front view, standing, *harai*   Photo 6: right side view, *harai*

Move the left knee to the right heel, kneel and swing the sword overhead.

During the swing overhead the blade moves from the blocking position directly to the high position. It does not swing around the left shoulder. After the left hand grasps the hilt, adjust the right grip.

Photo 7: front view, standing,
sword moving to vertical

Photo 8: right side view,
sword moving to vertical

Photo 9: front view, kneeling, *jodan*

Photo 10: front view, kneeling, downward cut

Advance the right foot and cut downward at the enemy.

Perform blood-cleaning.

Sheath the sword.

INAZUMA (Lightning)

General Description

稲妻

The enemy makes a downward center cut from the high position. Stepping back you cut at his exposed right forearm. Kneeling, cut the enemy down from the high position.

Commentary

This is the third form that details a response to an attack from the front. This trio, composed of *Yokogumo*, *Tora Issoku*, and *Inazuma*, can be thought of as "transitional forms." That is, they resemble forms found in the First Tradition and aid the practitioner in making the transition to the Middle Tradition.

In *Seichu To* in the First Tradition, you counterattacked a standing enemy. Here you do so again. This time, though, the direction of attack is changed and more importantly, the distance has been reduced.

You have neither the time nor space to step forward. In a way this is fortunate, because the backward step from *tate hiza* is easier than the sideways rising step in *Seichu To*.

Movements

Photo 1: front view, *tate hiza*

Sit facing the front in the drawn-up knee position.

Photo 2: front view, *tate hiza,* initiating horizontal draw

Photo 3: front view, *tate hiza,* right knee vertical

- Since the enemy presses his attack, immediately grip the sword with both hands.

- Raise the right knee.

- Pull the left foot back one step.

- Draw the sword and cut upward at the enemy's forearms.
  Rise while drawing. The sword edge is flat, or slants a little to the right. The point moves smoothly through the arc.

Swing the sword overhead in the flowing parry, kneel and move the left foot to the right heel.
While swinging the sword overhead in the flowing parry, the sword point hangs down in the right fist. Twisting the sword to the left, clearly protect the left shoulder.

Advance the right foot and cut down the enemy.

Perform the blood-cleaning.

Perform the sheathing.

Photo 4: front view, standing, forearm strike

Photo 5: left side view, standing, forearm strike

UKIGUMO (Floating Clouds)

General Description

Your enemy sits very close to your right side. He reaches over your knee and attempts to seize the hilt of your sword. Rising, pull away and draw at his chest; bring down the enemy to the rear, using both hands on the sword. Finally, cut down at the fallen enemy.

Commentary

The first three forms in this Tradition make an easy transition from the previous one. This form, *Ukigumo*, introduces the complexity and sophistication that are characteristic of the Eishin Ryu and the Middle Tradition.

Previously the swordsman dealt with enemies from outside his personal group. In this form the enemy is sitting right beside him. He is, perhaps, justified in being surprised, but by now, we have learned that a swordsman can take nothing for granted.

The steps of this form are designed to move your body to an attacking position within a very small space. You neither have time to move far enough away to use more familiar techniques, nor do you want to. You must remove this enemy as quickly as possible.

The sword work is more intricate. Following a sideways draw, there is a gripped-blade slice. Gripped-blade techniques are regarded as coming from older, more combat-oriented sources.

The method of swinging the sword to the high position is also new. In previous forms you usually rotated the sword around the left shoulder. In *Ukigumo* the sword is reversed in front of the right shoulder by throwing the point upward. The left hand can easily grip the reversed hilt and move the sword overhead. This is a more direct transition, but requires more strength.

Movements

Photo 1: front view, *tate hiza*

Sit with the front on your right, in the drawn-up knee position.
The enemy is sitting immediately on your right side, facing the same direction.

- Since the enemy attempts to seize your sword hilt, grip the scabbard with your left hand and pull the sword over to the left hip; press the right hand against the right waist.

- Raise the right knee to vertical.

Photo 2: front view, *tate hiza,* left hand
pulling scabbard away

Photo 3: left side view, left hand pulling
scabbard away

Photo 4: front view, kneeling,
scabbard at left waist

Quietly stand and move the left foot one large step to the left, further removing the hilt from the enemy.

Point your right foot directly at the enemy. Turn your face so you are looking at him.

Photo 5: front view, standing,
scabbard at left waist

Photo 6: left side view, standing,
scabbard at left waist

- Move the left foot across the front in a semi-circle so that it arrives to the right outside of the right foot.

- Using the left hand, lift the sword over the enemy's head, pulling it around to your right waist and your waiting right hand.

  This places the left foot very close to the enemy's left thigh. To accomplish this, both knees must bend. The left foot must stand on tiptoe. The left calf crosses in front of the right shin. This is said to resemble sagi ashi *(the legs of a heron).*

Photo 7: front view, standing,
left foot crossing

Photo 8: left side closeup, feet

Photo 9: front view, standing, left foot crossing, initiating draw

- Grasp the hilt with the right hand and draw the sword to the right side, attacking the enemy's chest and right arm.

- Twist the hips to the left, turning the upper body in that direction, and pull the scabbard to the left waist.

- Turn the left foot over as the attack finishes.
  Time the leftward twist with the left-hand pull on the scabbard as the point is drawn. Both knees bend more deeply to accommodate the twist. The left foot

Photo 10: front view, standing, draw

Photo 11: left side view, standing, draw

turns over; turn the arch of the foot up and roll the top of the instep onto the floor. At the end of the draw, the right fist is near and a little below the right hip. The blade is turned flat, and slants upward toward the enemy's right shoulder.

Photo 12: left side closeup, feet

Photo 13: front view, *iaigoshi*,
left hand on blade

- Turn the left foot back over.
- Pull back the right foot a large step to the right rear.
- Extend the left hand and grip the back of the blade.
  Twist the hips back to the right. Do not let the sword shift from its current position. In gripping the back of the blade with the left hand, pinch the blade ridge firmly between the thumb and the base of the middle finger.

Photo 14: front view, kneeling,
left hand on blade

- Continue the backward pull of the foot into a kneel, bringing the right knee to the floor.
- Using the continued twist of the hips, cut the enemy down to the right by slicing against his chest.
  During the movements of the back-step and slice, the upper body twists strongly to the right. Slice the sword to the right, raising the right hand, so that the point slants down. At the end of the movement the right fist is about the height of the right shoulder. The right elbow is bent; the left stretches out straight. The edge faces the right.

Photo 15: front view, kneeling, slice

Photo 16: front view, kneeling, end of slice

- Remove the left hand from the blade.

- Using the right hand, and turning the sword a little to the front, throw the point high over the right shoulder.

- Move the sword to the high position diagonally over the right shoulder, re-gripping with the left hand on the way.

- Move the right knee to the left heel, turning the right foot to the left.
  This is a new form of swinging the sword overhead, in which the sword is kept on the right side. The right fist rises above the right shoulder. The sword travels diagonally to the left, to the high position in a straight line.

Photo 17: front view, kneeling, left hand removed from blade

Photo 18: front closeup, rotated blade

Photo 19: front view, kneeling, sword diagonally over right shoulder

Photo 20: front view, kneeling, left *jodan*

Photo 21: front view, kneeling, downward cut

- Turning the left foot to the right, step heavily on the fallen enemy's arm.

- Avoiding your left knee, cut down at the enemy's body.
  The hands will finish the cut outside of the left knee.

Perform blood-cleaning.

Sheath the sword.
At the proper moment pull the left foot back to the right thigh, and turning, face the front.

YAMAOROSHI (Mountain Wind)

General Description

The enemy sits to your right, facing in the same direction. He grips his sword with both hands, preparing to draw it. You step on his left thigh, pinning him, and strike his right hand with your hilt. You draw at his chest, then force the enemy down backwards and cut downward at his body.

Commentary

This form, together with the previous one, *Ukigumo*, gives you a pair of examples of action that can be taken against an enemy on your right side.

The footwork in *Yamaoroshi* is not so intricate as in *Ukigumo*, but it is more sophisticated than that the First Tradition.

The sword is again applied with a sideways draw, a gripped-blade technique and a kneeling cut. The overhead swing is again accomplished by throwing the point high over the right shoulder and moving directly to the high position.

An interesting feature of this form is the initial step onto the enemy's left thigh. This step effectively immobilizes him, because it prevents him from shifting his weight off his left foot. Such a step would be just as effective if done to an enemy sitting in *seiza*.

The form also introduces the use of other parts of the sword than the blade as a weapon. In this case, *Yamaoroshi* uses a hilt strike.

Photo 1: front view, *tate hiza*

Movements

Sit with the front on your right, in the drawn-up knee position.

The enemy is assumed to be sitting immediately adjacent to your right, facing the same direction.

- The moment the enemy puts both hands on his sword, grip your sword with your left hand, thumb on the guard.

- Place your right hand at your right waist.

- Look squarely at the enemy.

Photo 2: front view, *tate hiza,* grasp scabbard w/ left hand, looking to right

- Raise your right knee and, pivoting on the left knee, turn 90-degrees to face the enemy.

- Turn the sword and scabbard upside down and lift the hilt up toward your face. *The blade will now be facing down. The left hand will be about chest height.*

Photo 3: front view, kneeling, hilt to face

Photo 4: front closeup, kneeling, left hand

- Stamp strongly down on the enemy with your right foot, pinning his left thigh.
- Strike a hard blow to the enemy's right hand with the end of the upside down hilt.

Photo 5: front view, kneeling,
stamp and strike

Photo 6: left side closeup,
strike at enemy's right hand

Photo 7: front view, kneeling, hilt lift

Lift the hilt up and push it down to the right, bringing the guard close to the right waist and the hilt to your waiting right hand.

Lift the hilt as you pull it to the right, so the end passes close to your nose. The right foot remains on the enemy's thigh.

Photo 8: front view, kneeling,
hilt drop into right hand

Photo 9: front closeup, right hand

- Draw the sword to the right, attacking the enemy's chest and right arm, pulling the scabbard back to the left rear.

- Twist the hips to the left.

- Pivoting on the left knee, turn the left shin 90-degrees toward the right heel. *The edge is now flat. It passes over your right thigh. In practice, simulate the draw by stopping sharply. At the end, the blade will angle up. The right fist will be in the neighborhood of the right hip. The right and left heels come close together. All this time the right foot still pins the enemy's thigh.*

Photo 10: front view, kneeling, draw to right   Photo 11: right side view, draw to the right

- Release the scabbard and grip the blade with the left hand.

- Pivoting on the left knee, turn the left foot 90-degrees back to the left. *Do not disturb the position of the sword. The left foot will return to approximately its position before the draw. The right foot is still on the enemy's thigh.*

Photo 12: front view, kneeling,   Photo 13: left side view, left hand on blade
left hand on blade

Photo 14: front view, kneeling, slice

- Again pivoting on the left knee, turn the whole body, with the right foot, 90-degrees to the right.

- Using the left and right hands, cut the enemy by slicing to the right. *The right foot finally steps off the enemy's left thigh. You will be facing about 180-degrees to your original sitting position. The right foot will be parallel to the left shin and foot. This slice has a scooping motion. At the end of the cut, the sword will be pointing downward. The right elbow will be about shoulder height. The sword point will be about 25cm. above and to the front of the right foot.*

- Releasing the left hand, swing the sword to the upper right, re-grip, and move to the high position.

- Stamp the right foot down one step forward, to pin the fallen enemy's left arm. *This is similar to the sword reversal in* Ukigumo. *Toe the right foot in, approximately 60-degrees to the left.*

Photo 15: front view, kneeling, left hand
removed from blade

Photo 16: front closeup, rotated blade

Photo 17: front view, kneeling, sword diagonally over right shoulder

Photo 18: front view, kneeling, *jodan*

- From the high position, cut downward at the fallen enemy's body.

- Pivoting on the ball of the right foot, twist the body 90-degrees to the left. *The left knee is lifted and pulled around to the rear. The cut coincides with the knee dropping back to the floor.*

In this posture, perform the blood-cleaning.

Sheath the sword.
Pull back the right heel to the left thigh.

Photo 19: front view, kneeling, downward cut

Photo 20: left side view, downward cut

IWANAMI (Waves Breaking Against Rocks)

General Description

The enemy sits immediately to your left, facing in the same direction. When he turns toward you, forestall his attack by striking his left hand. Then thrust forward, piercing his solar plexus. Bring down the enemy by slicing at his back. The form finishes with a downward cut at the enemy's body.

Commentary

In this form the swordsman again faces an enemy at close quarters. We have already seen that this does not guarantee friendliness.

Iwanami introduces, not only footwork against a leftward opponent, but the thrust. In addition to the cut and the slice, the sword can be thrust into the enemy's body, somewhat as in European fencing. Thrusts can be either one or two-handed, vertical or horizontal. In this case, the thrust is vertical, powered by the right hand and guided by the left.

The form also utilizes a hilt strike, as in *Yamaoroshi,* and uses the overhead swing and cut found in that form.

Movements

Photo 1: front view, *tate hiza*

Sitting with the front on your left, in the drawn-up knee position, you are immediately adjacent to your enemy, who is on your left facing the same direction.

- Slide your left foot directly back while rising to a kneeling position.

- Grip the sword with both hands and begin drawing to the front.

- Watch the enemy intently.
  The left knee does not leave the ground. The sword is drawn edge up.

Photo 2: front view, kneeling,
draw to knee, looking to the left

- As the enemy turns to face you, pivot on the left knee, and turn 90-degrees to the left to face him.

- Forestall the enemy's attack by striking the back of his left hand with your hilt, in the vicinity of the fourth finger.

Photo 3: front view, kneeling, strike to hand

Photo 4: left side view, kneeling, strike to hand

- Draw the sword through a arc, from the left side, upward past the face, and down to the right, gripping the blade with the left hand at the end.

- The instant the point leaves the scabbard, pull the right foot back to the left knee.
  When the turn ends, the right fist will be along side the right hip, the left hand will be along side or slightly in front of the right knee. The sword will be horizontal, pointing at the enemy. The edge will be downward.

Photo 5: front view, kneeling,
draw passing face

Photo 6: left side view, kneeling,
draw passing face

Photo 7: front view, kneeling,
left hand on blade

Photo 8: right side view, kneeling,
left hand on blade

- Stamp the right foot down one step forward.

- Thrust horizontally into the enemy's solar plexus.

- Immediately pull out the sword.
  During the thrust, the left hand remains fixed at the right knee. The right hand thrusts. During the extraction, the left hand remains at the knee. The right hand alone pulls back.

Photo 9: front view, kneeling, thrust

Photo 10: right side view, kneeling, thrust

Having extracted the sword, raise it in both hands and extend it deeply along the enemy's right side.

The edge rotates to horizontal.

Photo 11: front view, kneeling,
deep extension

Photo 12: right side view,
kneeling, deep extension

Pivoting on the left knee 90-degrees to the right, cut the enemy by slicing from behind his right side.

This slicing movement is the same as in Yamaoroshi. *Clearly turn the right foot 90-degrees as the body moves.*

Photo 13: front view, kneeling, slice

Photo 14: right side view, kneeling, slice

- Releasing the left hand, turn the sword over to the upper right and re-grip, moving to the high position.

- Stamp the right foot forward.
  You are assumed to be stepping on the enemy's right arm. Toe the right foot in.

Photo 15: front view, kneeling, sword
diagonal over right shoulder

Photo 16: right side view, kneeling, sword
diagonal over right shoulder

Photo 17: front view, kneeling, *jodan*

Photo 18: right side view, kneeling, *jodan*

- Pivoting on the ball of the right foot, turn 90-degrees to the left, facing the enemy squarely.

- At the same time, cut downward at the enemy's chest.
  This is the same movement as in Yamaoroshi.

In this position, perform blood-cleaning.

Sheath the sword, pulling the right heel back to the left thigh.

Photo 19: front view, kneeling, downward cut

Photo 20: left side view, kneeling, downward cut

UROKOGAESHI (Repeating Pattern)

General Description

The enemy sits on your left, facing in the same direction. You draw at his temple, then immediately cut downward at his head.

Commentary

This form, together with Iwanami, forms a pair dealing with an enemy on the swordsman's left. Thus we have two pairs, Ukigumo and *Yamaoroshi,* and *Iwanami* and *Urokogaeshi,* that give techniques for both sides.

This technique is nearly the same as that of the *Sa To* form in the First Tradition, except that in that form the draw is done from a kneeling posture, and this technique is done from the half-kneeling, half-standing posture.

The form is called *Gaeshi* (repeating) because it uses techniques already seen in the First Tradition.

Movements

Photo 1: front view, *tate hiza*

Sit with the front on your left, in the drawn-up knee position.

Photo 2: front view, *iaigoshi*,
horizontal draw

- Pivoting on the ball of the right foot, turn 90-degrees to the left into the half-sitting, half-standing posture, facing the enemy and pulling the left foot to the rear.

- Draw at the enemy's temple.
  The withdrawal of the left foot produces the necessary distance for drawing the sword.

Move the left knee to the right heel, kneeling, and swing the sword overhead.

Photo 3: front view, *iaigoshi*, sword over left shoulder

Photo 4: front view, kneeling, *jodan*

Advance the right foot one step and cut downward at the enemy's forehead.

Perform blood-cleaning.

Sheath the sword, pulling back the right foot.

Photo 5: front view, kneeling, downward cut

NAMIGAESHI (Repeating Waves)

General Description

The enemy is sitting behind you, facing the same direction. You turn left 180-degrees, to draw at his temple. Immediately, you cut downward at the enemy's head.

Commentary

This form continues the progression of the enemy's position. We have had him in the front, on the left and right, and now he is in the rear.

This form is nearly the same as the *Atari To* in the First Tradition, except that the draw is done from the half-kneeling, half-standing posture.

Movements

Photo 1: front view, *tate hiza*

Sit with the front at your rear, in the drawn-up knee position.

Photo 2: front view, *iaigoshi*, horizontal draw

- While drawing the sword, pivot on the ball of the right foot and turn 180-degrees left, into the half-sitting half-standing posture, by pulling the left leg around.

- Draw at the enemy's temple.
  Turn while drawing the sword. You should be done when about 2/3 of the blade is drawn.

Photo 3: front view, *iaigoshi*,
sword over left shoulder

Place the left knee on the floor, even
with the right heel and swing the sword
overhead.

Photo 4: front view, kneeling, *jodan*

Photo 5: front view, kneeling, downward cut

Advance the right foot one step and cut
down at the enemy's forehead.

Perform the blood-cleaning.

Sheath the sword, as in the Returning
Pattern.

TAKI OTOSHI (Dropping Waterfall)

General Description

The enemy is sitting to your rear, facing the same direction. He grips the butt of your scabbard. You shake him off and thrust at his chest. You then cut him down at the forehead.

Commentary

This is the second form dealing with a rear attack. It is characteristic of the Middle Tradition that forms are given mostly in pairs.

This form returns to the complicated footwork of the Eishin Ryu, using the heron leg stance. The draw that is combined with this stance is a new technique. The blade is edge up and drawn nearly vertical back along your left side.

A thrust is used as the initial counterattack. It is delivered edge up directly from the drawing position.

Photo 1: front view, *tate hiza*

Movements

Sit with the front to your rear, in the drawn-up knee position.

• When the enemy seizes the butt of your scabbard with his right hand, without immediately resisting, grip your scabbard with your left hand, thumb on the guard.

• Press the right hand to the right waist.

Photo 2: front view, *tate hiza*, left hand on scabbard, looking over left shoulder

Photo 3: right side closeup, hands

Photo 4: front view, standing,
looking over left shoulder

- Pull the left foot straight back toward the enemy and rise, looking to the left so you can see him.

- Pull the scabbard to the right in your belt to adjust for this turn, but offer little resistance.
  Look backward over your left shoulder. The enemy will have to stand and lean forward to keep his grip, but be careful not to jerk him forward.

Photo 5: front view, standing

Photo 6: right side closeup, left hand

- Suddenly, turn the left fingers up, and twisting, raise the sword upward in the direction of the left shoulder.

- The left foot swings to the right, passing over the right foot until the calf touches the shin.
  This motion twists the scabbard from the enemy's grasp. The edge faces the front. Do not place the left foot on the floor.

Photo 7: front view, standing, freeing sword

Photo 8: right side view, standing,
freeing sword

Photo 9: right closeup, feet

- Grip the hilt with the right hand.
- Stamp the left foot, out of the one-legged stance, down to the right side of the right foot.
  Toe out with the left foot.

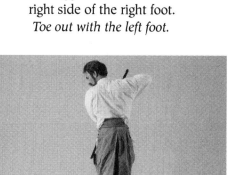

Photo 10: front view, standing,
right hand on hilt

Photo 11: right side view, standing,
right hand on hilt

Photo 12: right side closeup, feet

- Immediately stamp the right foot down about 30 cm. to the right of the left foot.

- Draw the sword a little upward to the right side.
  These two quick steps should make some noise. Pull back the right hand to shoulder height to accomplish the draw. The sword will be nearly vertical, edge up. You are now fully facing the enemy.

Photo 13: front view, standing, draw

Photo 14: right side view, standing, draw

- Pivot the right foot on its heel and point the toes in the same direction as the left.

- Glide-step toward the enemy with the left foot.

- From the sword's position, thrust into the enemy's chest.
  This is a single-handed thrust, with the edge up.

Photo 15: front view, standing, thrust

Photo 16: right side view, standing, thrust

Photo 17: front view, standing,
sword passing left shoulder

Swing the sword overhead in the flowing parry.

Photo 18: front view, standing, downward cut

Advance the right foot one step and cut downward at the enemy's forehead.

Immediately kneel on the left knee and perform blood-cleaning.

Sheath the sword.

Photo 19: front view, dropping to left knee,
sword moving to right

Photo 20: right diagonal view, dropping
to left knee, sword moving to right

Photo 21: front view, kneeling,
end of *eishin chiburi*

NUKI UCHI (Sudden Attack)

General Description

You sit facing your enemy, in close proximity. Perceiving his malicious intention, you quickly draw your sword and cut him down.

Commentary

Here, again, we find the swordsman in close proximity to his enemy. If he thought himself safe, he is rudely surprised.

This is the only form in the Middle Tradition performed from *seiza*. It is similar to the *Nuki Uchi* in the First Tradition. It is characteristic of the Muso Shinden Ryu that each of its Traditions ends with such a form. You will find a similar one at the end of the Inner Tradition.

Although the movements of the knees are identical to the *Nuki* Uchi of the First Tradition, the draw is different. Previously you used a horizontal draw and then swung the sword around the elbow to the high position, making the following cut. Now you will use a vertical draw and go immediately to the cut. Consequently, the action is much faster. It also requires less room.

You should practice this form quickly, as in the First Tradition, so that the movements do not break up into individual pieces.

Movements

Sit formally facing the front.

Photo 1: front view, *seiza*, sword settled

Photo 2: front view, kneeling on both knees, vertical draw

- Suddenly, grip the sword with both hands, and draw upward along the left side.

- Spread the knees apart.

- In one stroke swing the sword overhead in the flowing parry.

- Add the left hand to the hilt.

- Lift the knees and bring them together.

Photo 3: front view, knees in air, *jodan*

Photo 4: front closeup, knees

- Cut downward at the enemy's forehead.

- The knees separate and strike the floor.

Photo 5: front view, kneeling on both knees, downward cut

Perform the *Eishin Ryu* blood-cleaning.

Sheath the sword.
Close the knees at the end.

5. The Inner Tradition: The Oku Jai
(Seated Techniques)

BACKGROUND

The Inner Tradition of the *Muso Shinden Ryu* is the third set of forms, taught after the study of the *Eishin Ryu*. As such, it is regarded as more difficult than the *Omori Ryu* or the *Eishin Ryu*.

The Inner Tradition has both seated and standing forms. The eight seated forms will be described in this chapter. All begin from the drawn-up knee sitting position. This position is basic to the Middle Tradition.

The forms are designated by name. Sometimes a second name is also given. The forms are:

> **Kasumi** (Mist); *muko barai* (beating the other)
>
> **Sunegakoi** (Enclosed Shin); *tsuka dome* (hilt stop)
>
> **Shihogiri** (Four Directional Cut); *shi sumi* (four corners)
>
> **Tozume** (Enclosing Doors); *mi sumi* (three corners)
>
> **Towaki** (Side Door); *muko zume* (the other enclosed)
>
> **Tanashita** (Lower Shelf)
>
> **Ryo Zume** (Both Enclosed)
>
> **Tora Bashiri** (Rushing Tiger)

The descriptions that follow will use the same form as in the previous chapter. The other usual conventions of the descriptions will still be followed. Unless otherwise noted, the downward cut is delivered with both hands.

DISTINCTIVE FEATURES

In the First Tradition the forms used a single-step forward to define the drawing interval: the distance needed to reach the enemy with the sword. The Middle Tradition often defined the drawing interval with a single-step backward. In the Inner Tradition both the forward and backward step from the drawn-up knee position are used.

The cutting actions that follow the draw often involve more complex steps than previously.

The forms of the Inner Tradition, like those of the two preceding traditions, are assumed to take place indoors, but the Inner Tradition stresses this location more than the others. Many of the forms assume that the practitioner must move in and around a typical Japanese room.

The blood-cleaning of the Inner Tradition is the same as that of the Middle Tradition. Care must be taken that it is conducted to demonstrate remaining heart.

The sheathing is also the same. The back of the blade is placed at the scabbard mouth in the vicinity of the center of the blade, and the sword is sheathed by pulling it to the right in a single movement, until the point slips into the scabbard, and then inserting at a moderate speed. When the sword is about 20 cm to 25 cm from finishing, the sheathing stops and then continues to a quiet ending, demonstrating remaining heart.

In the seated techniques of the Inner Tradition the footsteps on rising are quiet. This is said to demonstrate the *musei no kiai* (soundless spirit meeting).

KASUMI (Mist); *muko barai* (beating the other)

General Description

Your first enemy sits facing you at the front about 1.5 meters away. Before he can attack, you draw, aiming at his temple. Turning over the sword you cut at his neck. You then cut down the enemy from the high position, and finish the form with blood-cleaning and sheathing.

Commentary

Here, again, we have a transitional form. The initial position, *tate hiza*, is familiar from the Middle Tradition. The horizontal draw is also known.

The forward right step, rather than the backward left step, differentiates this form from ones previously studied. It requires that the weight be kept on the left knee, rather than shifted forward. As a result, the step is much faster.

Techniques in the Inner Tradition are generally more straight forward than in the Middle Tradition, but are also more rapid and require more accuracy.

This form could be used against two opponents who attack you sequentially from the front.

Movements

Photo 1: front view, *tate hiza*

Sit facing the front in the drawn-up knee position.

Photo 2: front view, *tate hiza*, initiating horizontal draw

Sensing the enemy's hostile intentions, rise on the left knee, advance the right foot one step forward, and draw the sword, striking the enemy's temple.
This is essentially the same draw as in the Shohatto *form of the First Tradition.*

Photo 3: front view, *tate hiza,*
right knee vertical

Photo 4: front view, kneeling,
large horizontal draw

Turn over the right hand, reversing the blade.

Photo 5: front view, kneeling,
sword turned over

Photo 6: right side closeup, right hand

Photo 7: front view, kneeling,
left horizontal cut

- Slide the left knee to the right heel.
- Cut back to the left, striking the neck of the second enemy.
  The sword movements should look as though you are cutting a trail through mist.

Again turn the right hand over, reversing the blade and immediately swing the sword overhead.

Photo 8: front view, kneeling, sword turned over

Photo 9: right side closeup, right hand

Photo 10: front view, kneeling, sword passing left shoulder

Photo 11: front view, kneeling, *jodan*

Photo 12: front view, kneeling, downward cut

Advance the right foot one step and cut downward at the enemy's forehead.

Perform blood-cleaning.

Sheath the sword, pulling back the right foot.

SUNEGAKOI (Enclosed Shin); *tsuka dome* (hilt stop)

General Description

This form is nearly identical to Tora Issoku *in the Middle Tradition. The enemy, seated in front of you, attacks your right foot. You first stop the enemy's sword. Making use of his retreat, you cut him down from the high position.*

Commentary

Here the swordsman is faced with an enemy who attacks first. He must consider defense if he is to survive. The swordsman chooses the beat as his defensive technique.

As noted, this form is nearly identical to *Tora Issoku*. It differs only in that you must react more quickly. In *Tora Issoku* you moved immediately to the beat because the enemy had drawn and was cutting at your right foot. Here, you must respond while the enemy is drawing.

To constrain him from drawing rapidly, you draw your own sword hilt directly at his right hand. This slows him, but doesn't stop him. He still draws and cuts at your right leg.

You move directly to the beat. Recall that this requires you to grip the hilt from the top, with your thumb down the side. It also requires that you adjust this grip later when swinging the sword overhead.

Movements

Sit facing the front in the drawn-up knee position.

- As the enemy draws to cut at your right foot, raise the right knee toward vertical and pull the left foot one step backwards.

- Draw the sword, aiming your hilt at the enemy's right hand.
  This confines his movement.

Photo 1: front view, *tate hiza*   Photo 2: front view, *tate hiza*, initiating horizontal draw

Photo 3: front view, *tate hiza,*
right knee vertical

Photo 4: front view, standing,
draw til point emerges

Clearly preserving your right leg, ward off the enemy's sword with your sword
blade ridge.

This is the same warding off movement that appears in the Tora Issoku *form in
the Middle Tradition.*

Photo 5: front view, standing, *harai*

Photo 6: right side view, *harai*

Move the left knee to the right heel, while kneeling, and swing the sword
overhead.

Advance the right foot and cut downward at the enemy.

Perform blood-cleaning.

Sheath the sword.

SHIHOGIRI (Four Directional Cut); *shi sumi* (four corners)

General Description

There are four enemies to the front and rear, left and right. You draw and attack the rear, right, left, and front enemy in turn. You finish the form with blood-cleaning and sheathing.

Commentary

So far we have seen the swordsman in situations with, at most, two enemies. The implication is that, while one or two persons might prove treacherous and attack, there would not be a general battle.

Of course this would not always be the case. A swordsman could be set upon by any number of people and have to fight his way out. In this form he is surrounded and must deal with four opponents.

The order of his counterattack is rear, right, left and front. This order is chosen because it removes the most dangerous enemies first.

The rear enemy is the most dangerous because he cannot be seen. The right enemy is next because his draw is the quickest and shortest. The left enemy is next because he is at the rear when the swordsman turns to attack the right enemy. The front enemy is last because he's the only one left.

The initial counterattack is a thrust, this time delivered horizontally. The other enemies are dispatched with downward cuts. The footwork is straight forward, involving a series of pivots on the left knee.

You cannot assume that each of your enemies will wait his turn to attack you. Once you have killed the rear enemy they will all attack, being watchful that they don't get in each other's way.

While you are counterattacking each enemy, you must be aware of what the others are doing. Watch them out of the corners of your eyes.

The techniques of this form serve the basis of using the sword when enclosed by a large number of enemies. The techniques can be used against opponents at the corners as well.

Movements

Photo 1: front view, *tate hiza*

Sit facing the front in the drawn-up knee position.

Photo 2: front view, *tate hiza,*
initiating horizontal draw

- Rising to the left knee, step forward strongly with the right foot.

- Draw the sword slanting to the front. *Rotate the sword to horizontal. Do not pull back the scabbard.*

Photo 3: front view, kneeling,
draw til point emerges

Photo 4: front view, kneeling,
sword horizontal at left side

Sliding the right foot toward the left knee, pierce the left chest of the rear enemy, thrusting horizontally past your left arm.

Rotate the upper body to the left as needed.

Photo 5: front view, kneeling, rear thrust, looking over left shoulder

Photo 6: left side view, kneeling, rear thrust, looking over left shoulder

Photo 7: front view, kneeling, sword passing left shoulder

Step the right foot about 90-degrees to the right and swing the sword overhead in a flowing parry at the left side.

Add the left hand and cut downward at the right enemy.

Photo 8: front view, kneeling, *jodan*

Photo 9: front view, kneeling, downward cut

Immediately step the right foot 180 degrees to the left and swing the sword overhead in a flowing parry at the right side.

Photo 10: front view, kneeling, looking back

Photo 11: front view, kneeling, sword passing right shoulder

Photo 12: front view, kneeling, *jodan*

Photo 13: front view, kneeling, downward cut

Cut downward at the left enemy.

Again step 90-degrees to the right and swing the sword overhead in a flowing parry at the left side.

Photo 14: front view, kneeling, sword passing left shoulder

Photo 15: front view, kneeling, *jodan*

Cut downward at the forehead of the front enemy.

Photo 16: front view, kneeling, downward cut

Perform blood-cleaning.

Sheath the sword.

TOZUME (Enclosing Doors); *mi sumi* (three corners)

戸
詰

General Description

There are two doors in front, to the left and right. These suddenly open revealing two enemies at the forward diagonal directions. You draw and attack the right enemy first, and then cut down the left enemy. The form finishes with blood-cleaning and sheathing.

Commentary

The interior doors of a Japanese house, called *fusuma* (door), are solid panels 3 feet by 6 feet. There is a lintel at 6 feet containing the upper sliding track for the door.

When the door is opened by the enemy, he is seriously constrained. If he is standing, the height of the lintel prevents him from attacking with a vertical draw and cut. Either standing or kneeling, the narrow width of the doorway prevents the use of a horizontal draw. To press his attack the enemy must either drop to one knee and cut vertically, or step through the doorway. Either of these moves will take time.

The swordsman is already sitting. He needs only to rise to his knee and attack with a vertical draw and cut. Hence, in spite of being out-numbered, he has the advantage.

The enemy in the right doorway is attacked first, for the usual reason. If he is standing, waiting to step though the doorway, you strike at his torso. If he is kneeling, preparing to attack after opening the door, you cut at his head.

You then pivot to attack the second enemy. Instead of turning on your left knee, you exchange knees and cut with the left knee forward. The exchange is best done by lifting the left knee and placing the right knee down on almost the same spot. It must be rapid and you cannot pause because of the pain.

When you attack the second enemy you can take a small glide-step forward with the left foot to adjust the distance.

Movements

Photo 1: front view, *tate hiza*

Sit in the drawn-up knee position with the front diagonally to your left.

Photo 2: front view, kneeling,
draw to point emerge

- As the first secret door opens, advance the right foot one step obliquely to the right front.

- Draw the sword vertically on the right side, and continuing the motion, cut downward single-handed at the right enemy.
The right foot can be assumed to cross the threshold.

Photo 3: front view, kneeling,
one-hand downward cut

Photo 4: front view, middle of turn,
sword passing right shoulder

- Immediately turn the body 90-degrees to the left, setting the right knee on the floor and raising the left knee.

- Swing the sword overhead in a flowing parry at the right side.

Photo 5: front side view, *jodan*

Photo 6: front view, kneeling, downward cut

Cut downward at the left enemy, emerging from the left door.

Perform blood-cleaning.

Sheath the sword.

TOWAKI (Side Door); *muko zume* (the other enclosed)

General Description

There is a door to your right front, in the wall on your right side, concealing an enemy who is waiting for an opportunity to strike. A second enemy advances from your left rear. Forestalling the first enemy, you draw and attack the second. Then you cut down the first enemy, still in his hiding place.

Commentary

The swordsman is sitting with a wall on his right. Just ahead of him is a door. An enemy approaches from the left rear. The door opens, revealing an enemy to the right front corner. Clearly, they hope to pin the swordsman between them.

There is a fundamental flaw in their strategy, though. Remember that the doorway constrains the enemy's attacks. The swordsman can keep the enemy in the doorway long enough to dispose of the enemy at the rear, who is more dangerous.

You use two techniques to constrain the enemy in the doorway. First, you step over the threshold of the door with your right foot. Standing on the lower sliding track, you prevent the enemy from shutting the door in your face. Second, you draw your hilt directly at the enemy, forcing him backwards if he wants to gain space.

While he is forestalled, you thrust at the second enemy's chest. Then you swing the sword into the high position and cut the first enemy down. Remember, you can do this because you are kneeling and can cut under the door lintel.

Movements

Photo 1: front view, *tate hiza*

Sit in the drawn-up knee position with the front diagonally to your right.

Photo 2: front view, *tate hiza,*
initiating horizontal draw

- When the hidden enemy, seeing the advance of the rear enemy, begins to open the secret door, advance your right foot strongly one step to the right front corner.

- Draw the sword with the blade horizontal, edge to the outside, directly at the hidden opponent.
The right foot is assumed to obstruct the door, preventing its closure. The draw forestalls the first enemy, preventing him from emerging. Do not move the scabbard.

Photo 3: front view, kneeling,
draw til point emerges

Pierce the left chest of the rear enemy, thrusting horizontally over your left arm.
Rotate the upper body to the left as needed.

Photo 4: front view, kneeling, rear thrust,
looking over left shoulder

Photo 5: left side view, kneeling, rear thrust,
looking over left shoulder

- Rotate the upper body back to the front.
- Swing the sword overhead at the left side.

Photo 6: front view, kneeling,
sword passing left shoulder

Photo 7: front view, kneeling, *jodan*

- Scoop the right foot to the left and return it to the floor.
- Cut downward at the enemy.
  The slight scoop of the right foot is assumed to push the door open, exposing the hidden enemy.

Photo 8: front view, kneeling, downward cut

Photo 9: front view, kneeling, downward cut

Perform blood-cleaning.

Sheath the sword.

TANASHITA (Lower Shelf)

General Description

The enemy is to your front, but your advance is obstructed by the edge of a low shelf. You creep forward under this obstruction, and suddenly appear, cutting the enemy down. The form finishes with blood-cleaning and sheathing.

Commentary

Items in Japanese houses are stored in different ways. Some things are put into closets having the same kind of doors as are used to divide rooms. Some goods are kept in chests or cabinets, called *tansu* (chest of drawers). Some items are kept on shelves, called *tana* (shelf). Items are also placed on shelves for display.

The shelf in this form is one of the display type. It is in the room proper, attached to one of the walls, perhaps at a corner. In any event, the swordsman cannot advance without going around, over or under it. He chooses to go under, to surprise his enemy.

The enemy is known to be dangerous. Because the shelf obstructs the path, the enemy cannot see the swordsman. He takes him by surprise when he emerges.

The techniques of this form could be applied to any low obstruction. They could also be done in the dark to take the enemy by surprise.

Movements

Sit in the drawn-up knee facing the front.

Photo 1: front view, *tate hiza*

Draw the sword while advancing the right foot a large step to the front.

Draw the sword straight, without rotating the blade. Use more emphasis on the rear pull of the left hand than on the advance of the right foot. Lower the head and upper body. Keep the hips low.

Photo 2: front view, *tate hiza,* initiating horizontal draw

Photo 3: front view, kneeling, draw til point emerges

Photo 4: left side view, kneeling, draw til point emerges

Photo 5: front view, crouching, fully extended draw

Photo 6: left side view, crouching, fully extended draw

Carry the sword from the left side to the back.

Photo 7: front view, crouching,
sword on back

Photo 8: left side view, crouching,
sword on back

Slide the left knee to the right heel.
Keep the body as low as possible. You are assumed to be going under the shelf.
Place the left hand on the hilt, and let the hilt precede you.

Photo 9: front view, kneeling,
sword on back

Photo 10: left side view, kneeling,
sword on back

Advance the right foot and raise up.

This step is assumed to carry you beyond the obstruction. In practice, the preceding and this step can be repeated before rising to simulate a long shelf.

Photo 11: front view, kneeling, *jodan*

Photo 12: left side view, kneeling, *jodan*

Photo 13: front view, kneeling, downward cut

Cut down at the enemy.

Do not lift the hands from in front of your face when cutting. The sword hilt moves in a circle, forward and down.

Perform blood-cleaning.

Sheath the sword.

RYOZUME (Both Enclosed)

General Description

Both you and your enemy are enclosed in a space so narrow that it does not allow freedom to draw the sword as is usually done. You draw, adjusting for the narrowness, and attack the enemy with a thrust. You then cut the enemy down, finishing with blood-cleaning and sheathing.

Commentary

Since this is a seated form we assume it takes place in doors. The narrow space, then, must be some part of a house, perhaps a corridor or other kind of passage. What the swordsman is doing sitting in a corridor is not known. Perhaps he is waiting for permission to enter a room.

In any case, he is now constrained by exactly the same circumstances that previously hampered his enemy. The choice of counterattack technique is severely limited. The horizontal draw is unusable, as is the standing vertical draw and cut. The kneeling vertical draw and the thrust can still be used, so the form focuses on these techniques.

Movements

Photo 1: front view, *tate hiza*

Sit facing the front in the drawn-up knee position.

Advancing the right foot slightly, draw the sword to the right front.

Photo 2: front view, *tate hiza*,
initiating horizontal draw

Photo 3: front view, *tate hiza*,
draw til point emerges

Photo 4: left side view, *tate hiza*,
draw til point emerges

- Rise up on the left knee.

- Turning the sword over with the right hand, bring the hilt to rest in front of the navel and grasp it with the waiting left hand.

Photo 5: front view, kneeling,
sword reversing

Photo 6: left side view, kneeling,
sword reversing

Photo 7: front view, kneeling,
sword at navel

Photo 8: left side view, kneeling,
sword at navel

- Advance the right foot.
- Thrust with both hands at the front enemy.

Photo 9: front view, kneeling, thrust

Photo 10: left side view, kneeling, thrust

Withdraw the sword and swing it overhead.
   This is not done with a flowing parry, but with a much more direct manner.

Photo 11: front view, kneeling, *jodan*

Photo 12: left side view, kneeling, *jodan*

Cut downward at the enemy's forehead.

Perform blood-cleaning.
Because of the narrowness, the blood-cleaning is done with small movements.

Photo 13: front view, kneeling, downward cut

Photo 14: front view, kneeling,
end of *eishin chiburi*

Sheath the sword.
Because of the narrowness, the sheathing is done to the front, with the edge up.

Photo 15: front view, kneeling, beginning *noto*

Photo 16: left side view, kneeling,
beginning *noto*

Photo 17: front view, kneeling, point entry

Photo 18: left side view, kneeling, point entry

Photo 19: front view, kneeling, end of *noto*

Photo 5: front view, standing,
horizontal draw

Photo 6: front view, *iaigoshi*,
sword at right waist

- When the correct drawing interval has been gained, step suddenly forward with a large right step.

- Raise up the upper body and draw horizontally at the enemy.

Lower the left knee and cut down the enemy from the high position.

Perform the blood-cleaning.

Sheath the sword.
Draw the right foot near the left.
Draw the hilt near the right waist,
while half-crouching.

Because another enemy attacks from the front, while the sword is still 5 to 6cm out, pull the left foot back one step, into the half-sitting, half-standing posture.

Photo 7: front view, *iaigoshi*,
sword at right, left foot forward

Fall back before the enemy with
the same small hurrying steps.

Photo 8: front view, standing,
horizontal draw

When the correct drawing interval has
been gained, pull the left foot back in
a large step and draw horizontally to
the front.

Kneeling on the left knee, swing the
sword overhead, and cut down the
enemy.

Perform blood-cleaning.

Sheath the sword.

6. The Inner Tradition: The Oku Iai

(Standing Techniques)

BACKGROUND

Thirteen forms comprise the standing technique section of the Inner Tradition, although the last form is actually done from the formal sitting position. Some have subtitles, in addition to the more usual title. They are:

Yuki Tsure (Accompanying)

Tsuredachi (Together)

So Makuri (All Rolled Up); *goho giri* (five direction cut)

So Dome (All Stopped); *hanashi uchi* (disengaging strike)

Shinobu (Faithful Husband); *yoru no tachi* (long sword in the night)

Yukichigai (Crossing)

Sodesurigaeshi (Returning from Brushing the Sleeve);
ken no koto (circumstantial wisdom)

Mon Iri (Entering the Gate); *kakure sute* (hide and discard)

Kabe Zoi (Adjusting for the Wall); *hitonaka* (in public)

Ukenagashi (Flowing Parry); *yorumi nuki* (relaxed draw)

Oikakegiri (Pursuing Cut)

Ryoshi Hikitsure (Both Warriors Brought Together)

Itomagoi (Farewell Visit); *nuki uchi* (sudden attack)

DISTINCTIVE FEATURES

Several of the standing forms take place outside, in a typical Japanese urban environment. The practitioner must understand not only the structure and layout of a Japanese house, but also the neighborhood in which it is likely to be found.

The blood-cleaning and sheathing are, unless otherwise noted, the same as in the seated forms.

YUKI TSURE (Accompanying)

General Description

While you are walking, two enemies catch up and fall in step with you, on the left and right sides. They intend to take you away to some unwanted destination. Before they are in control of the situation, you attack, first the enemy on the right and then on the left. Finish the form with blood-cleaning and sheathing.

Commentary

The swordsman finds enemies on either side. They have made no hostile move, but he knows they are dangerous. Falling in on either side is an obvious tactic to control an opponent. It allows control of an opponent, while avoiding an open confrontation. It is used by police forces even today.

You do not wait to get to wherever they are taking you. Instead, you suddenly stop. As the enemies swing around to face you, dispatch them. Start with the right enemy because he is the more dangerous.

Movements

Step forward with the left foot.
   This simulates walking, and is the moment the enemies fall in step with you.

Before stepping forward with the right foot, deliberately pause.
   You are unexpectedly letting the enemies go one step past you. They will turn to face you to see what is happening.

Photo 1: front view, standing, *bukezukuri*

Photo 2: front view, standing, *bukezukuri*, left foot forward

Photo 3: front view, standing, initiating vertical draw

- Step to the right side with the right foot.

- With the right hand draw and cut downward at the top of the right enemy's left shoulder with the priest's stole cut.
  A Buddhist priest's stole is a rectangle of cloth that is worn from the left shoulder to the right armpit. The priest's stole cut is made from the top of the left shoulder (or the right) slanting to the lower diagonal direction. A reversed priest's stole cut is made upward along the same path.

Photo 4: front view, standing, vertical draw to the right diagonal

Photo 5: front view, standing, one-hand leftward slanting cut

Photo 6: front view, standing,
sword passing right shoulder

Quickly turn and face the left enemy.

Photo 7: front view, standing, *jodan*

- Slide the left foot toward the left enemy.

- From the right side swing the sword overhead in a flowing parry motion.

- Add the left hand to the hilt.

Photo 8: front view, standing, downward cut

Cut down at the enemy's forehead from the high position.

Perform blood-cleaning.

Sheath the sword, pulling back the left foot.

TSUREDACHI (Together)

General Description

As in the first form, Yuki Tsure, *you are again between two enemies, who fall in step with you on the left and right sides. You seize control, attacking, first the enemy on the left and then on the right. You finish the form with blood-cleaning and sheathing.*

Commentary

Here, again, you do not wait until you get to wherever they are taking you. Rather than lag behind, though, in this form you step ahead, pressing in on the right enemy.

The right enemy is the more dangerous, for the usual reasons. However, instead of attacking him directly, you choose to hamper him and attack the left enemy.

Initially you are all facing the same direction. When you step into the right enemy, he will move away from you, turning to see what you are doing. Because you stepped toward the right, the left enemy is now partly behind you, and has taken on added importance because of this new position. You must attack him immediately, using a rear thrust. You must then return to the first enemy before he has a chance to attack.

Movements

Step forward with the left foot.
   This simulates walking and is the moment the enemies fall in step with you.

Photo 1: front view, standing, *bukezukuri*

Photo 2: front view, standing, *bukezukuri*, left foot forward

Photo 3: front view, standing,
initiating horizontal draw to the right

- Advance the right foot a small step to the right front.

- Draw the sword to the right side in a single stroke.
  The step places you close to the right enemy, which inhibits him. Keep your eyes fixed on him. The blade is horizontal, edge to the outside. Do not pull the scabbard back.

Photo 4: front view, standing,
draw to right til point emerges

Photo 5: front view, standing,
rear thrust, looking to left

As the sword point separates from the scabbard, quickly look at the left enemy and thrust at the right side of his chest over your left arm.

Turn to the left as needed.

Photo 6: front view, standing,
sword passing left shoulder

- With the feet as they are, quickly turn rightward to again face the right enemy.

- Swing the sword overhead.

- Add the left hand.

Photo 7: front view, standing, *jodan*

Photo 8: front view, standing, downward cut

- Slide the right foot to the front.

- Cut down at the enemy's forehead from the high position.
  The enemy has pulled away from you to gain distance.

Perform blood-cleaning.

Sheath, pulling back the right foot.

SO MAKURI (All Rolled Up); *goho giri* (five direction cut)

General Description

You respond to five enemies coming at you serially from the front. You finish the form with blood-cleaning and sheathing.

Commentary

The swordsman, as noted in the commentary on *Shihogiri* in the seated forms of the Inner Tradition, could not depend on having only one opponent. He must also be able to deal with many enemies. In *Shihogiri* he had four surrounding him. In this form he has five, coming at him serially.

A serial attack is not improbable. In-doors, enemies coming down a corridor, or through a doorway, would have to attack one at a time. Out of doors, a narrow path, the space between houses, or an opening in a crowd would produce the same effect.

This form uses five different cuts, and a smooth method of repeatedly swinging the sword overhead. It can be considered as teaching the basic techniques for dealing with a large number of opponents.

Movements

Photo 1: front view, standing, *bukezukuri*

- Pull back the right foot one step to the rear.

- Draw the sword upward and swing it overhead in a left flowing parry. *The first enemy comes from the front, crowding in to cut at you. The back step and flowing parry ward off the attack.*

Photo 2: front view, standing,
initiating vertical draw

Photo 3: front view, standing,
sword passing left shoulder

- Advance the right foot.
- Add the left hand and cut at the left side of the enemy's head.

Photo 4: front view, standing,
left hand added

Photo 5: front view, standing,
left slanting cut

- Advance the left foot.
- Swing the sword overhead from the right side.

Photo 6: front view, standing, end of cut

Photo 7: front view, standing,
sword passing right shoulder

Photo 8: front view, standing, *jodan*

As the second enemy advances, cut at his right shoulder in the priest's stole cut.

- Advance the right foot.

- Swing the sword toward the right shoulder.
  This position, reminiscent of the eight-phase posture, is called katsugi
  (carry on the shoulder).

Photo 9: front view, standing,
rightward slanting cut

Photo 10: front view, standing, *katsugi*

Cut the left torso of the third enemy in a shallow, slanting cut.

Photo 11: front view, standing,
slanting *do giri*

Photo 12: front view, standing,
slanting *do giri*

Turn the sword horizontal, point to the left rear.
This will cause your wrists to cross.

Photo 13: front view, standing,
sword pointing to left

Photo 14: left diagonal closeup, hands

- Advance the left foot.
- Cut with both hands in a sideways single stroke at the right side of the fourth enemy's body.

Photo 15: front view, standing, horizontal cut

Photo 16: front view, standing, horizontal cut

- Advance the right foot.
- Swing the sword overhead to the high position past the right side.

Photo 17: front view, standing,
sword pointing to rear

Photo 18: front view, standing,
sword passing right shoulder

Photo 19: front view, standing, *jodan*

Photo 20: front view, standing, downward cut

Cut downward at the fifth enemy's forehead.

Perform blood-cleaning.

Sheath, pulling back the right foot.

SO DOME (All Stopped); *hanashi uchi* (disengaging strike)

General Description

Your freedom of movement is constricted on both sides. In front are several enemies, who must attack one at a time. You respond to them, but show no hostility, being willing to cease after each one. Finally, when finished, you do a narrow blood-cleaning and sheathing.

Commentary

The swordsman is attacked sequentially by several enemies, as in *So Makuri*. Rather than respond with hostility to them all, he chooses to hold no grudges and to be willing to stop after each. It is up to the opponents to press the attack.

The narrowness of the situation can be the result of the physical layout or other factors. For example, the area may be a narrow bridge, an embankment, or a narrow street. The swordsman might also be attacked in a crowd, where there is only a narrow opening between people.

The counterattack is a single-handed vertical draw and cut. The left hand is used to control the scabbard. The heron leg stance is used to show a willingness to stop.

Movements

Photo 1: front view, standing, *bukezukuri*

- Confronting the first enemy, advance the right foot and point the toes to the left.

- Twist the hips to the left, so that only half the body is presented, and point the left toes to the left.

- Draw upward with the right hand and cut down the enemy.

Photo 2: front view, standing, initiating
elongated vertical draw

Photo 3: front view, standing,
elongated vertical draw

Photo 4: front view, standing, elongated
one-hand downward cut

Photo 5: left side view, elongated
downward cut

Begin to sheath the sword.
This sheathing is very elongated. Touch the back of the blade to the scabbard mouth at a point about 1/3 from the tip. Draw the sword slowly to the front until the tip enters.

Photo 6: front view, standing,
sword on left hand

Photo 7: front view, standing,
sheath to point entry

Photo 8: left side view, standing,
sheath to point entry

- Move the left foot a very small step forward, just in front of the right foot, with the toes pointing to the left.

- Continue to slowly sheath the sword.
  This is the heron leg step previously encountered. Only the toes touch. The shins cross. The hips move twist. Use this motion to continue to sheath the sword, moving the scabbard forward. The sword will be 1/3 to 1/2 inserted. It is this motion that shows your willingness to "disengage."

Photo 9: front view, standing,
continue sheathing

Photo 10: left side view, standing,
continue sheathing

Suddenly, confronting the second enemy, repeat the attack as before.

Repeat the sheathing as before.
In this way, deal with a sequence of enemies. Only two would be necessary to demonstrate the form.

Finally, perform blood-cleaning.
The sideways movement is restricted by the narrowness of the location.

Sheath the sword, pulling back the right foot.
This sheathing is very elongated. Touch the back of the blade to the scabbard mouth at a point about 1/3 from the tip. Draw the sword slowly to the front until the tip enters. Then insert the blade in a straight line to the rear.

SHINOBU (Faithful Husband); *yoru no tachi* (long sword in the night)

General Description

This form takes place at night, in a dark room. The enemy is in front, facing in your direction and advancing cautiously. You cannot see each other. You lure him into attacking, but avoid being struck, and strike him down instead. You finish the form with blood-cleaning and sheathing.

This form's title is a word play on the adverb shinobu *(stealthily).*

Commentary

Illumination in a Japanese house was provided by floor lanterns, using either candle or oil lamp. When these are extinguished for sleep, and the doors closed to contain warmth, windowless rooms can be very dark.

It is reasonable that the swordsman and his opponent cannot see each other. Instead, they strain their ears to hear the other, trying to discover his position.

Speed is not your problem, noise is. In fact, you will move much slower than usual to prevent the enemy from hearing you.

You must draw your sword as quietly as possible. The blade must not rattle in the scabbard. You can pinch the blade between your left thumb and index finger as you draw it to eliminate noise.

You bend slowly over and scuff the floor, trying to make the sound of someone walking. When your opponent betrays his position by striking, you attack decisively.

Movements

- Faintly discerning the enemy, rotate your body to the left, carrying the left foot backward to the right rear.

- Slowly draw the sword, as quietly as possible.

Photo 1: front view, standing, *bukezukuri*

Photo 2: front view, standing, initiate draw

- Bend forward.

- Tap the sword point lightly on the floor two or three times with a circular motion. *Do not make hard taps, but rather scuff the floor. This sounds more like a moving person.*

Photo 3: front view, bending

Photo 4: front view, bending, sword tapping floor

Photo 5: front view, standing, *jodan*

- Rise up.

- Swing the sword overhead to the two-handed high position and wait.

Photo 6: front view, standing, downward cut

- When the enemy attacks the location of the sounds, advance the left foot to the left front.

- Cut down.

Perform blood-cleaning.

Sheath the sword, pulling back the left foot.

YUKICHIGAI (Crossing)

General Description

Two enemies advance from the front. One passes and attacks you from behind. You respond, attacking first the enemy at the front with a disabling blow, then the enemy to the rear, and then the front enemy again. You finish with blood-cleaning and sheathing.

Commentary

In this form the swordsman is placed between two enemies. This time, however, they are to the front and rear, rather than on each side. This placement, especially that of the enemy in the rear, makes the situation more dangerous and dictates the need for a very fast response.

The enemy in the rear would normally be the more dangerous and you would want to deal with him first. However, because he has to walk past you, turn and draw, you have a little time. This allows you to strike the front enemy with your hilt to forestall him before dealing with the rear enemy.

Movements

Photo 1: front view, standing, *bukezukuri*

- As one enemy passes you, deliberately enter into the space between the two men by stepping forward with the right foot.

- Strike with your hilt at the face of the front enemy.
  In the hilt-strike, both hands stretch out, carrying the sword and the scabbard forward. Strike the front enemy with the butt of the hilt just below his nose.

Photo 2: front view, standing, hilt strike

Photo 3: left side view, standing, hilt strike

Immediately, pull the scabbard to the rear with the left hand, leaving the hilt in place, drawing the sword.

Photo 4: front view, standing, draw til point emerges, looking over left shoulder

Photo 5: left side view, standing, draw til point emerges

- As soon as the point leaves the scabbard, rotate 180 degrees to the left, facing the rear enemy.

- Thrust to the enemy's chest.
  The blade is horizontal, edge up.

Photo 6: front view, standing, thrust

Photo 7: left side view, standing, thrust

- Rotate 180-degrees to the right.

- Swing the sword overhead to the two-handed high position, over the left shoulder.

Photo 8: front view, standing,
sword passing left shoulder

Photo 9: left side view, standing,
sword passing left shoulder

Photo 10: front view, standing, *jodan*

Photo 11: front view, standing, downward cut

Cut down at front enemy's forehead.

Perform blood-cleaning.

Sheath, pulling back the right foot.

SODESURIGAESHI (Returning from Brushing the Sleeve); *ken no koto* (circumstantial wisdom)

General Description

袖
摺
返

You see your enemy at the other side of a crowd. Using the form's movements, you pass through the crowd and cut down the enemy. You finish with blood-cleaning and sheathing.

Commentary

One would think that a crowd, seeing an armed swordsman moving toward an enemy, would tend to disperse, but this is not always the case. Some people might flee, some might drop to the ground, some might run straight into his path, but most would stand frozen. Imagine a crowd today, seeing a gunman in their midst.

The swordsman, then, must make his way through the crowd as unobtrusively as possible. At the same time, he must try not to injure any bystanders. Yet he must also arrive at the other side, prepared to cut down his enemy.

Sodesurigaeshi solves this problem. As you move through the crowd, your drawn sword is carried at your left side, edge up. Bystanders are unlikely to blunder into it; they are even unlikely to notice it until you've passed.

Upon confronting your enemy, you swing the sword in a wide circle, edge still up. Bystanders will scatter or be pushed aside. At the very end of the arc you suddenly swing the sword overhead, adjust the grip and cut down the enemy.

Movements

Step forward with the left foot.

Quietly draw the sword, edge up, straight forward.
   Keep your eyes on the enemy.

Photo 1: front view, standing, *bukezukuri*

Photo 2: front view, standing,
draw til point emerges

Photo 3: front view, standing, arms crossed

- Step forward with the right foot.
- The right fist moves below the left elbow; the left fist moves below the right elbow.
  Leave the sword as it is, edge up, pointing to the rear, and step forward into position along side it. The left and right forearms cross at your chest.

Photo 4: front view, standing, arms crossed, left foot forward

Step forward with the left foot.

- Step forward with the right foot to confront the enemy.

Photo 5: front view, standing, beginning sweep

- Open both arms in a large, horizontal sweep, carrying the sword to the right side.
  The sweep of the arms pushes the crowd aside. The blade is still edge up, so it does not injure anyone.

Photo 6: front view, standing, sweep

Photo 7: front view, standing, end of sweep

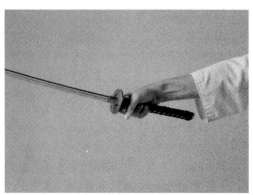

Photo 8: front closeup, right hand

Rotate the hands and swing the sword overhead to the two-handed high position, using a flowing parry motion on the right side.

• Step forward with the right foot to confront the enemy.

Photo 9: front view, standing,
arms extended, sword rotated

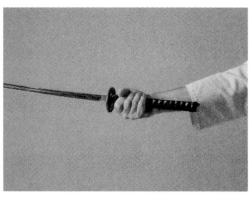

Photo 10: front closeup, standing, right hand

Photo 11: front view, standing,
sword passing right shoulder

Photo 12: front view, standing, *jodan*

Photo 13: front view, standing, downward cut

Cut down the enemy.

Perform blood-cleaning.

Sheath.

MON IRI (Entering the Gate); *kakure sute* (hide and discard)

General Description

While walking you see two enemies waiting ahead. One is inside a gate in a wall or fence on your left, and one waits outside on your right. You attack the one inside first, and then the one outside. You finish with blood-cleaning and sheathing.

Commentary

Japanese houses are usually not built perpendicular to the street. Instead, they are placed on their lots according to the principles of geomancy. The result is a ragged street line, with houses at many angles.

Japanese builders tend to use any space left available on the lot for gardens, and to enclose the whole property with a fence or wall. The entrance to the grounds must be made through a gate. These gates are often substantial, with roofs and benches inside.

Your enemy is hiding inside one of these gates. While you are distracted by the opponent outside, he will strike you from behind. Clearly, the hidden enemy is the more dangerous. If you can forestall the other enemy, you can deal with the hidden one first.

Movements

Step so that the left foot comes down opposite the center of the gate.
Toe out the left foot.

Photo 1: front view, standing, *bukezukuri*

Photo 2: front view, standing, *bukezukuri*, left foot forward

Draw the sword to the outside right, pulling it horizontally across the chest.
The blade is horizontal, edge to the outside.

Photo 3: front view, standing, initiating draw, pulling sword to extreme right

Photo 4: front view, standing, draw across chest til point emerges

Photo 5: front view, standing, thrust

- Pull the right foot sharply to the right, and rotate the body 90 degrees to the left.

- Thrust, piercing the chest of the enemy inside the gate.
  The overhead beam that forms the lintel of the gate prevents you from cutting down the enemy inside.

Photo 6: front view, standing,
sword passing left shoulder

- Rotate 180-degrees to the right.
- Swing the sword overhead to the two-handed high position.

Photo 7: front view, standing, *jodan*

Photo 8: front view, standing, downward cut

Cut down the outside enemy.

Perform blood-cleaning.

Sheath.

KABE ZOI (Adjusting for the Wall); *hitonaka* (in public)

General Description

There is a wall on the left and right sides, restricting your freedom to use your sword. The enemy comes from the front. Adjusting for the restrictions, you cut him down, and finish with a restricted blood-cleaning and sheathing.

Commentary

The walls mentioned above are probably ones enclosing houses on opposite sides of a street, As noted before, Japanese houses are not placed regularly and the resultant streets are very winding. They are also often enclosed by walls or fences and the streets can be very narrow.

This form sets the general pattern for sword drawing in a narrow space. You cannot stretch out to the left or right side. Accordingly, it could be used to cut down an enemy who was in the middle of a crowd, without injuring others.

This is the third form that specifically deals with narrow areas or describes techniques to use in a crowd.

Movements

Step forward with the left foot.
  This simulates walking between the two walls.

Photo 1: front view, standing, *bukezukuri*

Photo 2: front view, standing, *bukezukuri*, left foot forward

Photo 3: front view, standing, feet together

Before moving the right foot, deliberately pause, then move the right foot to the left foot and make the feet even.

Photo 4: front view, standing, initiating vertical draw

- Stand up on your tiptoes.

- Draw the sword nearly straight up, swinging it overhead to a two-handed high position over the left shoulder. *Because of the restricted position, the sword point may drop behind the back after the left hand grasps the hilt.*

Photo 5: front view, standing, extreme vertical draw

Photo 6: front view, standing, left hand added

Cut downward, describing a large circle.
Remain on tiptoe. The sword point comes clearly low to the ground.

Perform a very narrow blood-cleaning.

The sword point stays as close to the ground as it was, and moves sharply sideways. You cannot move the sword beyond the width of your body. Remain on tiptoe.

Photo 7: front view, standing,
large downward cut

Photo 8: front view, standing,
end of narrow *eishin chiburi*

Photo 9: front view, standing,
sword on left hand

Sheath.

The sheathing is very vertical. You must control the scabbard. Carry the hilt above the head as you insert the point. As the sheathing finishes, lower the feet to the ground.

Photo 10: front view, standing,
point insertion

Photo 11: front view, standing, end of *noto*

UKENAGASHI (Flowing Parry); *yorumi nuki* (relaxed draw)

General Description

Moving from the front, an enemy crowds in, cutting directly at you. You respond by deflecting his sword and counterattacking. You finish with blood-cleaning and sheathing.

Commentary

This forms bears a marked resemblance to the Ryu To form in the First Tradition. However, because the enemy comes from the front the deflection is different.

In Ryu To, the standing enemy attacked from the left side. The deflection had to cover both the head and the left shoulder. In this form the enemy attacks directly downward from the front and the deflection must strongly resist this cut.

The resultant technique bears a strong resemblance to the deflection used in *Gyaku To* in the First Tradition. You must be prepared for the shock. Receive his blade on your sword blade ridge as close to the guard as possible. The right elbow takes some of the force; the rest must be dissipated downward over your left shoulder.

You carry the block immediately to the right by stepping in that direction. If this and the previous motion are continuous, the enemy's sword will carry through the deflection past your left shoulder.

You counterattack immediately, striking the opponent with the priest's stole cut. The target of the cut is the shoulder. In *Ryu To* it was the hip. Care must be taken to avoid confusion between these two forms.

Movements

Photo 1: front view, standing, *bukezukuri*

- Advance the left foot a small step forward, pointing the toes to the right.

- Draw the sword upward, slanting to the right.
  The left foot is nearly in front of the right. The draw finishes in the flowing parry, clearly protecting the head and shoulder.

Photo 2: front view, standing,
initiating vertical draw

Photo 3: front view, standing,
deflection over left shoulder

Photo 4: front view, standing,
sword passing left shoulder

- Carry the right foot slanting to the right front.
- Use the sword to slide through the flowing parry.

Photo 5: front view, standing, left hand added

- Point the tip of the left foot toward the enemy.
- Add the left hand to the hilt.

Photo 6: front view, standing,
leftward slanting cut

- Move the right foot even with the left, fanning the toes apart.

- Cut at the top of the enemy's left shoulder.
  Aim at the joint between the shoulder and the neck. Bend the knees during the strike.

Perform blood-cleaning.

Sheath.

Photo 7: front view, standing,
leftward slanting cut

OIKAKEGIRI (Pursuing Cut)

General Description

An escapee runs. You follow up with rapid steps, while drawing the sword. Catching him, you cut him down from behind.

Commentary

Normally, a cut from the rear is not done by a person of the swordsman class, or with the disposition of a swordsman. However, the circumstances require that you do so, and you must act without hesitation.

This is an older form, and is generally practiced less than the others. There is some evidence that, although it originally was a combat technique, it was abandoned some time in the past, and that the form, as now done, is an abridgement of the original. Only a general description of the movements is *given.*

Movements

- Take several small, hurrying steps in pursuit of the escaping enemy.

- During these steps draw the sword.
  Begin with the left foot. These steps are similar to those in the Tora Bashiri *form, of the Inner Tradition seated techniques. The draw is taken when the left foot is forward.*

Catching up with the enemy, straighten up, swing the sword overhead to a two-handed high position, and cut him down.
  The targets would be the neck, arm or torso of the enemy.

RYOSHI HIKITSURE (Both Warriors Brought Together)

General Description

The enemy is cornered at your left side. Because of his proximity, you must cut him down with a special strike, as he pulls away from you to gain distance.

Commentary

This is also an older form, and is not practiced. It is included here for reference. It may also, however, be an abridgement. Only a general description of the movements is given.

Movements

- Advance the left foot to the front.

- Draw the sword straight ahead.
  The blade is horizontal, edge facing to the left, toward the enemy. The point pauses at the left armpit.

Photo 1: front view, standing, *bukezukuri*   Photo 2: front view, standing, forward draw

Photo 3: front view, standing, left hand on hilt

- Advance the right foot.
- Add the left hand to the hilt.
  Leave the sword in place and move up beside it. The wrists cross.

Photo 4: front view, standing, horizontal cut

Cut at the enemy's right arm and torso.
This cut is a raking, slashing action, rather than a clean cut. The hands produce a pushing-pulling, scissoring motion.

Photo 5: front view, standing,
horizontal cut cut

ITOMAGOI (Farewell Visit); *nuki uchi* (sudden attack)

暇
乞

General Description

You are exchanging bows at the conclusion of a visit. Suddenly you perceive the person has become an enemy. While at some stage in the seated bow, you draw and cut the enemy down. The form finishes with blood-cleaning and sheathing.

Commentary

This is the final form in the Inner Tradition and the last of the Muso Shinden Ryu. It is the sole seated form in the standing section. Its inclusion here is probably to finish out the pattern of closing each Tradition with a seated form.

The form places the swordsman in one of his most vulnerable situations: executing the deep seated bow. This bow is done from *seiza*. The swordsman first lowers his eyes, then places both hands palm-down in a triangle on the floor in front of him, and lowers his body toward the triangle.

Somewhere during this bow, the supposed friend suddenly turns into an enemy. Even while bowing the swordsman finds no security.

Itomagoi should be practiced from three different beginnings. These correspond to the degree of depth you have performed in the initial bow. First, begin the counterattack just after you have lowered your eyes. Second, begin after you've placed both hands on the floor. Third, begin after you've bowed deeply.

The draw is taken from whichever position you choose. In each case, the sword is drawn out horizontally into the space between you and the enemy. This is the same draw as in *Nuki Uchi* in the First Tradition. The sword is immediately swung overhead to a very high two-handed position. The enemy is cut down from here.

The footwork, or more correctly the "kneework," is also the same as in *Nuki Uchi*. That is, the knees are spread apart as the sword is drawn, lifted from the floor and clapped together as you move to the high position, and re-spread and slammed to the floor as you strike.

Movements

Sit facing the front.

Photo 1: front view, *seiza*, sword settled

Photo 2: front view, seiza,
both hands on floor, bowing deeply

Begin the seated bow, choosing one
of the three positions for practice.

Photo 3: front view, *seiza*,
bowing, initiating draw

Without wasting motion by straightening
up, draw the sword to the right.

*The sword is drawn out horizontally
into the space between you. This is the
same draw as in the* Nuki Uchi *form
in the First Tradition.*

Photo 4: front view, *seiza*, bowing,
draw til point emerges

Photo 5: front view, kneeling
on both knees, sword drawn

Photo 6: front view, knees in air,
very high *jodan*

- Lift both knees from the floor and clap them together.
- Swing the sword overhead to a very high two-handed position, using a flowing parry motion around the left elbow.
  The sword seems almost vertical.

Photo 7: front view, kneeling on both knees, large downward cut

- Separate the knees and drop back to the floor.
- Cut down at the enemy's head in a large circle.
  The sword point comes clearly very low to the floor. The body remains on tiptoe.

Perform blood-cleaning.

Sheath.
  At the end of sheathing, lower the body back to the sitting position.

Part Three

Established Kata
of the Japanese
Federations

7. Kata of the All-Japan Fencing Federation

BACKGROUND

全
日
本
剣
道
連
盟
制
定
居
合

These *Seitei Kata* (Established Forms) were selected by a committee authorized by the *Zen Nihon Kendo Renmei* "zen nipon kendo remmei" (All-Japan Fencing Federation). Seven forms were selected in March 1968. Three additional forms were added in April 1980. They represent both forms from traditional systems and forms altered or created specifically for the Federation.

There are ten forms, in three categories. These are: formal sitting forms, drawn-up knee forms, and standing forms. The forms are designated by title as well as number, and have the usual subtitles.

Formal Sitting Forms:

Mae (Front); *shomen* (center)

Ushiro (Rear); *ushiro muki* (facing the rear)

Ukenagashi (Flowing Parry); *migi muki* (facing the right)

Drawn-Up Knee Forms:

Tsuka Ate (Hilt Strike); *shomen* (center)

Standing Forms:

Kesagiri (Priest's Stole Cut); *shomen muki* (facing the center)

Morotezuki (Two-Handed Thrust); *mae muki* (facing the front)

Sanpogiri (Three Direction Cut); *sammen o muki* (facing three centers)

Ganmen Ate (Strike Between the Eyes)

Soetezuki (Fixing Thrust)

Shihogiri (Four Direction Cut)

DISTINCTIVE FEATURES

The blood-cleaning in the Established Forms, unless otherwise noted, resembles that used in the First Tradition. The sheathing is the same as in the First Tradition.

PRELIMINARIES

Since these forms are standardized by the Fencing Federation throughout its schools, the beginning and ending formalities are also standardized.

Beginning Formality

The sword is carried to the practice area in the right hand, with the hilt to the rear and the edge downward.

Perform a standing bow on entry to the practice area.

Photo 1: front view, sword in right hand   Photo 2: right side view, sword in right hand

Pass the sword to the front and transfer it to the left hand, carrying it in the usual way.

Sit.

Do not set the sword on the floor.

Photo 3: front view, middle of pass

Photo 4: front closeup, hands

Photo 5: front view, sword in left hand

Photo 6: left side view, sword in left hand

Bring the sword to the front with the left hand, slanting down to the left.

Grasp the sword at the guard with the right hand, palm up.

Slide the left hand down the scabbard and raise it to horizontal.

| Photo 7: front view, right hand on sword | Photo 8: front view, sword horizontal |

Arrange the cords, if any.

Use the left hand to move the sword to the vertical, edge to the left, and stand the butt on the floor. Use the left hand to rotate the sword, edge turning toward you, all the way to the right. Use the left hand to straighten the cords to the left and then lower them along the scabbard. Use the left hand to rotate the sword again, edge turning away from you, all the way to the left. Then use the left hand to again raise the sword to chest-high horizontal, right hand palm up, left hand palm down.

This whole procedure frees the cords from the scabbard. The sword returns to the same position you started from, with the cords now trapped against the scabbard with the left thumb.

Photo 9: front view, left hand
standing sword vertical

Photo 10: front closeup, hands

Photo 11: front view, rotated scabbard

Photo 12: front closeup, hands

Photo 13: front view, left hand
drawing out cords

Photo 14: front view, left hand lowering cords

Photo 15: front view, rotating scabbard

Photo 16: front closeup, hands

Place the sword on the floor in front, edge away from you.

Bow formally.

If there are any cords, pick them up with the little finger of the right hand.

Photo 17: front view, sword on floor

Photo 18: front view,
right hand picking up cords

Photo 19: front view, sword horizontal

Lift the sword with both hands as usual, and insert it in the belt.

Photo 20: front view, sword inserted in *obi*

Photo 21: left side view, sword inserted in *obi*

Photo 22: front view, left hand
drawing sword to rear

Photo 23: left side view,
left hand drawing sword to rear

Photo 24: left side view view, sword inserted

If there are cords straighten them
out to the right with the right hand.
Tie them at the waist.

Photo 25: front view, drawing cords to right

Photo 26: right closeup, tying knot

Photo 27: right closeup, tying knot

Photo 28: front view, *seiza*, w/ sword settled

Photo 29: left side view, *seiza*,
w/ sword settled

Photo 30: front view, standing, *bukezukuri*

Stand and move to the waiting area or directly to the practice position.

Photo 31: front view, *seiza*, w/ sword settled

Ending Formality

With the sword in the belt, move to the appropriate area.

Sit.

Photo 32: front view, drawing cords to right

Untie the cords, if any, and hold the ends with the little fingers of the right hand.

Photo 33: front view, right hand withdrawing scabbard

Place the left hand over the scabbard and withdraw the sword slowly with the right.

As the butt of the scabbard comes free, stand it up in the front center, edge to the left.

Raise the left hand and rotate the scabbard, edge turning toward you, all the way to the right.

If there are cords they will rap around the scabbard.

Photo 34: front view, left hand
standing sword vertical

Photo 35: front closeup, hands

Photo 36: front view, rotated scabbard

Photo 37: front closeup, hands

If there are cords, reach between the scabbard and the loop of cords with the left hand. Take the cords from the right fingers with the left hand. Draw them back through the loop and draw them down the scabbard, tightening them around it.

Photo 38: front closeup,
left hand taking cords

Photo 39: front view, tying cords
around scabbard

Photo 40: front closeup,
tying cords around scabbard

Photo 41: front view, *seiza*,
sword on ground in front

Lay the sword down from here, across the front, with the hilt to the left, edge toward you.

Arrange the cords, if any.

Bow formally.

Re-grip the sword with the right hand and stand it up in the front center, edge away from you, letting any cords hang down.

Photo 42: front view, *seiza*, right hand griping sword

Photo 43: front view, *seiza*, right hand standing sword vertical

Photo 44: front view, *seiza*, left hand on sword butt

Grip the end of the scabbard with the left hand, catching any cords.

Photo 45: front view, *seiza*, sword carried in left hand at side

Slide the sword through the left hand to assume the usual carrying position and release the right hand.

Stand.

Move to the edge of the practice area.

Transfer the sword across the front to the right hand, holding it in the original reversed way.

Bow and leave the practice area.

Photo 46: left side view, standing, sword in left hand

Photo 47: front view, middle of pass

Photo 48: front closeup, hands

Photo 49: front view, sword in right hand

Photo 50: right side view, sword in right hand

MAE (Front); *shomen* (center)

General Description

This form is performed in the same circumstances as the Shohatto *form in the First Tradition. The movements of the feet and knees are the same, as the enemy is struck by drawing to the front and cut down with an overhead stroke.*

The blood-cleaning used is the one prescribed for the Established Forms. The ending movements of the feet are the same as in Shohatto.

Commentary

This form, or one very like it, is often found as the first form in many systems. Its movements are considered basic.

Movements

Perform the same movements as are described in the *Shohatto* of the First Tradition.

USHIRO (Rear); *ushiro muki* (facing the rear)

General Description

This form is the same as the Atari To *in the First Tradition.*

Movements

Follow the movements of the *Atari To*. Take care to maintain the proper angle in the blood-cleaning, as described above.

UKENAGASHI (Flowing Parry); *migi muki* (facing the right)

General Description

Sitting customarily, you find the enemy about 1.5 meters away on the left side, facing in the same direction. Suddenly he stands and attacks with a downward cut. Using a flowing parry, you deflect the enemy's sword while standing. You then cut down the enemy in a diagonal cut from the top of the left shoulder to the right side.

Commentary

This form is similar to the *Ryu To* form in the First Tradition in that both have an enemy on the left who stands and attacks; both respond with a leftward deflection; and both cut the enemy down with a priest's stole cut. However, the forms differ on the techniques of the footwork, the parry, and the final cut.

Most of the comments made for *Ryu To* apply here as well.

Movements

Photo 1: front view, *seiza*, sword settled

Sit with the front on your left.

Suddenly the enemy stands, draws, steps forward and cuts at your head.

Photo 2: front view, *seiza*, initiating
vertical draw, looking to left

- Turn your head toward the enemy.

- Rising up, advance the left foot a little
  to the right.

- Draw the sword overhead in the upper
  front direction.

- Deflect the enemy's sword diagonally
  off your sword blade ridge to the left.
  *The blade is high, clearly protecting
  your head and shoulder.*

Photo 3: front view, *seiza*, vertical draw,
looking to left

Photo 4: front view, kneeling,
deflection over left shoulder

- Advance the right foot to the inside of the left foot.

- Stand up.

- As the enemy's sword continues its momentum in the flowing parry, rotate your
  sword around your back.

- Face the enemy directly while placing the left hand on the hilt.
  The point circles around the left shoulder.

Photo 5: front view, standing, deflection

Photo 6: front view, standing,
sword passing left shoulder

Photo 7: front view, standing, left hand added

- Pull back the left foot to the rear.

- Cut downward diagonally at the top
  of the enemy's left shoulder.
  *The moment the downward cut is done,
  the hands stop in front of the navel.*

Photo 8: front view, standing,
leftward slanting cut

Photo 9: front view, standing,
leftward slanting cut

- With the right hand reversed as it is, quietly sheath the sword.
- Place the left knee on the floor.

Photo 18: front view, standing,
sword drawn to point entry

Photo 19: left closeup, point entry

Photo 20: front view, kneeling, end of *noto*

Stand up.

Make the feet even.

Detach the right hand from the hilt.

TSUKA ATE (Hilt Strike); *shomen* (center)

General Description

While seated in the drawn-up knee posture, two enemies are at your front and rear, intending to attack you separately. First, you strike the enemy at the front in the solar plexus with your hilt. Continuing, you pierce the second enemy's chest with a single-handed thrust. Finally, you cut down the first enemy.

Commentary

This form is the only one of the Established Forms that begins from the drawn-up knee posture, *tate hiza*. Because it uses a forward step during the initial draw, it is more like the forms in the Inner Tradition than those in the Middle Tradition of the Muso Shinden Ryu.

The front and rear enemies sit with you, nominally friendly. Then they show their treachery. The rear enemy is, of course, the more dangerous. If you forestall the front enemy long enough to dispatch the rear one, you stand a good chance of winning.

The hilt strike is similar to ones you've already studied.

Movements

Photo 1: front view, *tate hiza*

Face the front, sitting in the drawn-up knee posture.

Photo 2: front view, *tate hiza,* gripping sword

- Place both hands on the sword.
- Advance the right foot one step.
- Stand up on the left toes.
- Thrust the sword and scabbard together to the front, striking the enemy in the solar plexus with the end of the hilt.

Photo 3: front view, kneeling,
advancing right foot

Photo 4: front view, kneeling, hilt strike

Photo 5: left side view, kneeling, hilt strike

Pull the scabbard back with the left hand as far as you can, and free the sword point.

The blade is horizontal, edge to the outside.

Photo 6: front view, kneeling,
draw by withdrawing scabbard

Photo 7: left side view, kneeling,
draw by withdrawing scabbard

Photo 8: front view, kneeling,
sword horizontal along left arm

Thrust across your left arm at the rear enemy's chest.

Rotate the body on the left kneecap to the left as needed.

Photo 9: front view, kneeling, rear thrust,
looking over left shoulder

Photo 10: left side view, kneeling, rear thrust

Photo 11: front view, kneeling,
sword passing left shoulder

- Face the front enemy.
- Extract the sword and, in one motion, swing it overhead.
- Add the left hand on the hilt.

Photo 12: front view, kneeling, *jodan*

Photo 13: front view, kneeling,
low downward cut

Cut downward at the front enemy's forehead.

Perform blood-cleaning.
  Open to the right and perform the Eishin Ryu blood-cleaning, as in the Middle Tradition.

Sheath the sword.
  Pull the right foot back toward the left. Settle the body into a crouching posture, on the left knee.

Stand up.
  Make the feet even.

Detach the right hand from the hilt.

KESAGIRI (Priest's Stole Cut); *shomen muki* (facing the center)

袈
裟
切

General Description

While you are walking, an enemy advances from the front, crowding in to cut at you. You draw from underneath, cutting him from his lower right side in a reversed priest's stole cut. Then, cut downward at the top of his left shoulder in a normal priest's stole cut.

Commentary

This form begins the standing section of the Established Forms. It is one of only two examples in either the Established Forms or the Muso Shinden Ryu of the underhanded draw.

This draw is regarded as older than either the vertical or horizontal draws. It has its origin in the manner of wearing the sword used prior to *bukezukuri*. The sword was not worn thrust through the belt, but suspended from it. In this older style, the edge was downward. When drawn from this position the sword moves through an arc that is now simulated by the underhand draw.

This draw requires that you first turn the hilt and scabbard over so that the edge is down. The grip is then taken from the top of the reversed hilt, with the thumb down the side. The sword is drawn forward and upward, cutting the enemy in the reversed priest's stole cut.

A Buddhist priest's stole is a rectangle of cloth that is worn around the body from the left shoulder to the right armpit. In older fencing terms the name of this cloth became associated with a downward diagonal cut from the top of the left shoulder (or the right) across the body.

The reversed priest's stole is a cut from the lower side slanting upwards to the opposite shoulder.

Photo 1: front view, standing, *bukezukuri*

Movements

- Advance the left foot.
- Place both hands on the sword, and rotate it in the belt until it is edge downward.

Photo 2: front view, standing,
initiating underhand draw

Photo 3: front view, standing,
underhand draw and cut

- Advance the right foot.
- Draw the sword from its upside down position and cut the enemy from his lower right side in a single-handed reversed priest's stole cut.
  The point should enter his torso above is waist. At the end of the cut the right hand should be above shoulder height.

With the feet as they are, rotate your right hand to point the sword at the ceiling and put the left hand on the hilt.
The sword swings overhead.

Photo 4: front view, standing, sword horizontal in front of forehead

Photo 5: front view, standing, *jodan*

Photo 6: front view, standing, leftward slanting cut

Cut downward from the top of the enemy's left shoulder in a priest's stole cut.
During steps 1 through 3 the sword mustn't stop. At the end of the last cut the hands stop in front of the navel. The sword point should not move beyond the width of the body.

Photo 7: front view, standing, *hasso no gamae*

- Pull back the right foot.
- Raise the sword to the eight-phase posture.
  The sword guard is even with the mouth. Demonstrate remaining heart.

Photo 8: front view, standing,
end of *eishin chiburi*

- Detach the left hand and grasp the scabbard mouth.

- Step back with the left foot.

- Swing the sword down to the right in the blood-cleaning of the *Omori Ryu*, the First Tradition.

Photo 9: front view, standing, end of *noto*

Sheath the sword.

- Move the left foot to make the feet even.

- Detach the right hand.

MOROTEZUKI (Two-Handed Thrust); *mae muki* (facing forward)

諸
手
突

General Description

You are attacked by three enemies, two in front and one at the rear. You draw at the first enemy in the front, and then thrust into his chest. Continuing, you cut down the enemy at the rear. Finally, you cut down the third enemy in the front.

Commentary

This form uses a situation you have met before: more than one enemy attacking sequentially. As before this might occur in a corridor, a bridge, a street or through an opening in a crowd, wherever it is too narrow for the enemies to attack more than one at a time.

Normally the rear enemy would be the more dangerous of the trio. Some attempt would be made to forestall the first enemy in the front until the rear enemy could be dispatched.

In *Morotezuki*, however, this is not done. The enemy in the front is attacked while the enemy at the rear is ignored. The reason for this is not known.

The thrust that is used in this form is a two-handed one. Such a thrust was used in *Ryozume* in the Inner Tradition of the *Muso Shinden Ryu.*

Movements

* Step forward with the left foot.
* Put both hands on the sword.

Photo 1: front view, standing, *bukezukuri*

Photo 2: front view, standing, initiating draw

- Step forward with the right foot.
- Turn the body slightly to the left.
- Draw and cut to the right side of the first enemy's head.

Photo 3: front view, standing,
upward slanting draw

Photo 4: front view, standing, downward cut

- Move the right foot even with the left foot.
- Lower the sword to the middle position and place the left hand on the hilt.

Photo 5: front view, standing,
feet together, *chudan*

Photo 6: left side view, standing,
feet together, *chudan*

- Advance the right foot one step.
- Thrust with both hands at the first enemy's solar plexus.

Photo 7: front view, standing,
two-hand thrust

Photo 8: left side view, standing,
two-hand thrust

- Rotate 180-degrees to the left, facing the rear enemy.
- Swing the sword overhead.

Photo 9: front view, standing,
sword passing right shoulder

Photo 10: left side view, standing,
sword passing right shoulder

- Step forward with the right foot.
- Cut downward at the rear enemy's forehead.

Photo 13: front view, standing, downward cut

Photo 14: left side view, standing, downward cut

- Rotate 180-degrees to the left, facing the second front enemy.
- Swing the sword overhead.

Photo 15: front view, standing, sword passing right shoulder

Photo 16: right side view, standing, sword passing right shoulder

Photo 17: front view, standing, *jodan*

Photo 18: front view, standing, downward cut

- Advance the right foot.
- Cut downward at the second front enemy's forehead.

Perform blood-cleaning.
> *The feet stay as they are. The blood-cleaning is the normal one for the Established Forms.*

Sheath the sword.

Move the rear foot to make the feet even.

Detach the right hand.

SANPOGIRI (Three Direction Cut);
sammen o muki (facing three centers)

General Description

三
方
切

You are walking forward. The enemies come from three directions, the center, left and right, splitting their attack. You attack the right, then left, then center enemy in turn. You finish with blood-cleaning and sheathing.

Commentary

Here, again, you are faced with more than one enemy. Common practice says the one on the right is the most dangerous. If you turn toward him, the one on the left is behind you and must be dispatched next. The one in the front can be dealt with last.

The cuts are the usual downward ones. The method used during the turns to swing the sword into the high position varies with the direction of rotation.

When rotating to the left, the sword is swung past the right shoulder. When rotating to the right, past the left shoulder.

Movements

Step forward with the left foot.

Photo 1: front view, standing, *bukezukuri*

Photo 2: front view, standing, *bukezukuri*, left foot forward

Photo 3: front view, standing, initiating
vertical draw, looking to right

- Step forward with the right foot,
  even with the left.
  *Place no weight on the right foot;
  just touch the toes down lightly.*

- Advance the right foot to the right.

- Attack the right enemy with a single-
  handed overhead draw and cut.

Photo 4: front view, standing, vertical draw

Photo 5: front view, standing,
one-hand downward cut

- With the feet in this position, turn 180 degrees to the left and face
  the left enemy.

- Swing the sword overhead, using a flowing parry motion over the
  right shoulder.

- Put the left hand on the hilt.

Photo 6: front view, standing, sword passing right shoulder

Photo 7: front view, standing, left *jodan*

Photo 8: front view, standing, downward cut

Cut down at the left enemy's forehead.

- Move the right foot 90-degrees to the right and turn to face the front enemy.

- Swing the sword overhead, using a flowing parry motion over the left shoulder.

Photo 9: front view, standing, sword passing left shoulder

Photo 10: front view, standing, *jodan*

Photo 11: front view, standing, downward cut

Cut downward at the front enemy's forehead.

Photo 12: front view, standing, left *jodan*

• Pull the right foot back.
• Take the two-handed high position. *Demonstrate remaining heart.*

Photo 13: front view, standing,
end of *eishin chiburi*

Pull back the left foot.

• Detach the left hand and place it at the left waist.
• Swing the sword down from the high position to perform blood-cleaning.

Sheath the sword.

• Move the right foot to make the feet even.
• Detach the right hand.

GANMEN ATE (Strike Between the Eyes)

General Description

While walking you are attacked by two opponents, one to the front and one at the rear. Sensing his hostile intentions, you forestall the first enemy by striking him between the eyes with the butt of your sword. You then draw, turn and thrust into the second enemy's mid-section before he can draw. Continue turning and step forward, cutting downward at your first opponent. Finish the form by performing blood-cleaning and sheathing.

Commentary

Here, again, you are penned in between two opponents. The rear one is the more dangerous. As you have done many times, you forestall the enemy at the front, which gives you the time you need to dispatch the enemy at the rear.

Once again you use a thrust to kill the enemy at the rear. This is deliver by one hand, with the blade horizontal.

Mechanically, this thrust most resembles the thrust used in European fencing.

Movements

Stand motionless facing the front.

Photo 1: front view, standing, *bukezukuri*

Begin walking forward with the right foot. Step right, left, and right.

Photo 2: front view, standing, *bukezukuri*, right foot forward

Place both hands on the sword, in the customary drawing positions, as you take the left step.

Photo 3: front view, standing, initiating draw

As you take the next right step move the sheathed sword forward with both hands, edge up, and strike your first opponent smartly between the eyes with the butt.

Photo 4: front view, standing, hilt strike

Photo 5: left side view, standing, hilt strike

- Pull the left foot back a little.
- Leaving the right hand as it is, immediately withdraw the scabbard with the left hand, drawing the sword.

Photo 6: front view, standing, drawing sword by withdrawing scabbard

Photo 7: left side view, standing, withdrawing scabbard

- Just as the sword point leaves the scabbard mouth, pivot on the right foot to the rear.
- As you pivot, rotate the blade edge to the right so that it is flat.
- At the end of the pivot bring the sword to the right hip.

Photo 8: front view, standing, sword at hip

Photo 9: left side view, standing, sword at hip

- Step forward with the right foot.

- Thrust slightly upward into the second opponent's mid section.
  Fully extend your right arm. The hilt will lie beneath your forearm.

Photo 10: front view, standing, thrust

Photo 11: left side view, standing, thrust

Photo 12: front view, standing,
sword passing right shoulder

- Without hesitation pivot on your
  right foot to the left, facing your first
  opponent.

- Withdraw your sword from the second
  opponents body and swing it overhead
  to the high position using a deflecting
  motion.

- Just as the sword comes overhead
  add the left hand to the hilt.

Photo 13: front view, standing, *jodan*

Photo 14: front view, standing, downward cut

- Immediately step forward with the right foot.

- Cut downward at the enemy's forehead.

Perform blood-cleaning.
The feet stay as they are. The blood-cleaning is that of the Eishin Ryu *system.*

Sheath the sword.
The feet stay as they are.

When the blade is fully inserted, step forward with the left foot as far as the right foot.

Release the right hand.

Step backward to your original position, left foot first.

SOETEZUKI (Fixing Thrust)

General Description

While walking you are attacked by one opponent immediately to your left. Sensing his hostile intentions, you attack him by turning left to face him, drawing your sword and cutting single-handed downward through his right shoulder. You then follow this with a short thrust. Finish the form by performing blood-cleaning and sheathing.

Commentary

In this form you return to the single enemy. You see him in front of you as you are walking. He moves to pass you on the left side. You interpret this as a hostile move.

The Japanese swordsman wears his weapon on his left side, the scabbard extending to the left rear. When he passes a person walking toward him he would attempt to pass on the right. If the two swordsmen passed each other on the left, there would be a chance that their scabbards might touch.

Striking scabbards together in this way is called *saya ate* (scabbard strike). It was considered a great insult and was immediately followed by a fight, wherever it occurred.

Since your enemy has chosen to pass you on the left, he is deliberately courting the scabbard strike. You are correct to distrust him.

As you pass each other you step backwards to the right. Since your enemy probably intended to strike your scabbard with his own, he will pass very close. You need to step away to gain the necessary distance to draw and cut at him.

After cutting, you deliver a short thrust, holding the blade in your left hand. Gripped-blade techniques are the specialty of some systems of sword drawing. Such a technique is probably included in the Established Forms to give students some access to these systems.

Movements

Stand motionless facing the front.

Begin walking forward, right-left-right.

Photo 1: front view, standing, *bukezukuri*

Place both hands on the sword as you take the left step.

- As you take the right step, turn left by pivoting backward on your right foot, extending you left foot to the rear.
- Rotate the scabbard slightly outward and draw the sword forward and up.

Photo 2: front view, standing, initiating vertical draw

Photo 3: front view, standing, vertical draw

At the end of the pivot, turn the draw into a one-handed diagonal downward cut through your opponent's right shoulder to his left hip. *This should be done by rotating around the left shoulder. The transition should be smooth.*

Photo 4: left side view, standing, sword passing left shoulder

Photo 5: front view, standing,
one hand rightward slanting cut

Photo 6: front view, standing,
one hand rightward slanting cut

- Twist your upper body slightly to the right.

- With your right hand, draw the hilt smartly back to your right hip, edge downward.

- Toe outward with the right foot.

Photo 7: left side view, standing,
sword at hip

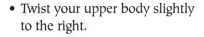

Place the palm of your left hand atop the back of the blade.

Hook you left thumb over the top. Pinch the blade between your left thumb and extended index finger. Point the blade at your opponent's mid-section.

Photo 8: front view, standing,
left hand on blade

- Step forward with the left foot.

- Deliver a short thrust into the opponent's mid-section.

- Draw up the right foot to reinforce the thrust.
  Do not change the position of your hand on the blade. Do not let the right hand move to the center line.

Photo 9: front view, standing, thrust   Photo 10: front view, standing, thrust

- With your left hand fixed as it is in space, slowly raise the hilt with your right hand diagonally upward to the right, while stepping forward with the right foot.

- Let the blade rotate under your left thumb and over your extended fingers.

Stop the right hand when it comes to chest level.
  The blade slopes downward to your left.
  Demonstrate remaining heart.

Photo 11: front view, standing,   Photo 12: left side view, standing,
    hilt lifting to right   hilt lifting to right

Detach your left hand from the blade and grasp the scabbard mouth.

- Take a deep step backward with your right foot.

- Perform blood-cleaning.
  Use the Eishin Ryu *style, but perform the action more gently than usual.*

Photo 13: front view, standing, end of *chiburi*   Photo 14: left side view, standing, end of *chiburi*

With both feet as they are, sheath the sword.

When the blade is fully inserted, step forward with the left foot as far as the right foot.

- Release the right hand.

- Turn right to face the front.

Step backward to your original position, left foot first.

SHIHOGIRI (Four Direction Cut)

General Description

While walking, you are attacked by four opponents, who approach you from the corners. You forestall the first opponent by striking the back of his right hand with your sword hilt. You then draw, turn and thrust into the second opponent's mid-section. Continue turning and step forward, cutting downward at the first enemy. You then continue turning and cut down the third and fourth opponents in turn. Finish the form by performing blood-cleaning and sheathing.

Commentary

This form has a slightly different flavor because the opponents are at the corners instead of the usual directions. You can see more of the two that are behind you. They are not quite as dangerous as usual.

This accounts for the order in which you face them. You first turn to the right corner to upset that enemy's draw. This places the enemy at the left rear corner directly behind you, so you must attack him next.

Once you have turned to the left rear to dealt with this enemy, the first enemy is now behind you. Fortunately, he is still stunned from your initial action. You turn back to him and finish him off.

There are two enemies left: one in the left front corner and one in the right rear corner. Because you are now facing to the right front corner, you can see both, one on your right and one on your left. The rightward enemy is the more dangerous, so you attack him next.

In doing so, you have turned your back on the last enemy, so you must immediate turn to him and finish the form.

Aside from the hilt strike to disable the first enemy, the form uses standard thrusting and cutting techniques.

Photo 1: front view, standing, *bukezukuri*

Movements

Stand motionless facing the front.

Begin walking forward, right-left-right.

Photo 2: front view, standing,
initiating draw

Place both hands on the sword as you take the left step.

- Take a right step by moving to the right front corner.
- Move the sheathed sword forward and upward with both hands, rotating the edge to the outside horizontal position.
- As your enemy grips his sword to draw, strike his right hand with your hilt.

Photo 3: front view, standing,
sword lifted for strike

Photo 4: front view, standing, hilt strike

Photo 5: front view, standing, draw sword
by withdrawing scabbard

- Leaving your right hand as it is, immediately withdraw the scabbard with your left hand, drawing the sword.
- Pull the left foot back a little and look over your left shoulder.

Photo 6: front view, standing, draw to release,
looking over left shoulder

Photo 7: front view, standing, thrust

- Just as the sword point leaves the scabbard mouth, pivot to the rear on the right foot.

- As you pivot, position the blade parallel to the ground, edge to the outside. *Bring the back of the blade against your body at chest level, pointing directly at the second opponent's mid-section. Because you initially stepped to the right front, all your orthogonal directions are really diagonal ones, relative to the practice area. This allows you to perform standard movements against diagonally placed opponents.*

- At the end of the pivot, glide step forward with your left foot.

- Deliver a one-handed straight thrust to the opponent's mid-section. *As you thrust, cross your arms, the left one under the right. Fully extend your right arm. The blade will slant slightly downward and the hilt will touch the underside of your right forearm.*

- Without hesitation, pivot to the right, facing your first opponent.

- Withdraw your sword from the second opponent's body and swing it overhead to the right high position using a deflecting motion.

- Just as the sword comes overhead add the left hand to the hilt.

Photo 8: front view, standing,
sword passing left shoulder

Photo 9: front view, standing, *jodan*

Photo 10: front view, standing, downward cut

- Immediately step forward with the left foot.
- Cut downward at the first opponent.

- Without hesitation, pivot 90-degrees to your right.
- Swing your sword overhead to a right high position.

Photo 11: front view, standing, sword passing left shoulder

Photo 12: front view, standing, right *jodan*

- Immediately step forward with your right foot.
- Cut downward at your third opponent.

Photo 13: front view, standing, leftward slanting cut

Photo 14: front view, standing,
sword passing right shoulder

- Quickly pivot 180-degrees to the left on your right foot.

- Swing your sword overhead to a high left position using a deflecting motion.

Photo 15: front view, standing, left *jodan*

Photo 16: front view, standing,
rightward slanting cut

- Without hesitation, step forward with your right foot.

- Cut downward at your fourth opponent.

Photo 17: front view, standing, *jodan*

- Step straight back with your right foot.
- Raise the sword to a left high position.

Photo 18: front view, standing, *chiburi*

- Step directly back with your left foot.
- Release your left hand from the hilt and press it against the scabbard at your waist.
- Perform blood-cleaning.
  Swing your blade downward in the First Tradition style.

Photo 19: front view, standing, end of *chiburi*

With both feet as they are, sheath the sword.

When the blade is fully inserted, step forward with your left foot as far as the right foot.

- Release the right hand.
- Turn right to face the front.

Step backward to your original position, left foot first.

8. Kata of the All-Japan Sword Drawing Federation

BACKGROUND

全
日
本
居
合
道
連
盟
制
定
居
合

These *Seitei Kata* (Established Forms) were selected by a committee authorized by the Zen Nihon Iaido Renmei (All-Japan Sword Drawing Federation) in October 1957. They represent forms most likely to be learned in the various systems, although not necessarily the most basic techniques were selected. Neither were they selected simply as winning techniques, but rather as most representative of the sword drawing principles of the systems.

There are five forms. The first two begin in the formal sitting position; the remaining three, from standing. They are designated by both title and by the systems from which they originate. They are:

Maegiri (Front Cut); *Eishin Ryu* (Excellent Faith System)

Mae Atogiri (Front-Rear Cut); *Mugai Ryu* (Nothing Excluded System)

Kiriage (Rising Strike); *Shinto Munen Ryu* (Way of the Gods and Impassive Mind System)

Shihogiri (Four Direction Cut); *Mizu Kamome Ryu* (Water Gull System)

Kisakigaeshi (Returning Sword Point); *Hoki Ryu* (Old Official System)

DISTINCTIVE FEATURES

When you deliver the final cut of each form you must say the word *eitsu* (an exclamation). This utterance is the final *kiai* (spirit meeting) of the form, and immediately precedes the demonstration of remaining heart.

The forms, unless otherwise noted, use the *Eishin Ryu* style of blood-cleaning.

The sitting and standing forms, unless otherwise noted, use the *Eishin Ryu* style of sheathing.

279

PRELIMINARIES

In addition to standardizing the forms, the sword drawing Federation has also standardized the beginning and ending formalities of practice.

Beginning Formality

Photo 1: front view, standing, sword carried in right hand

The sword is carried to the practice area in the right hand, with the hilt forward and the edge upward. The cords, if any, are held by the little fingers of the right hand.

Perform a standing bow upon entry to the practice area.

Sit.

Photo 2: front view, right hand standing sword vertical

Place the scabbard butt vertically to the right of the right knee.

If there are any cords, draw them away from the scabbard with the left hand. When they are free lower them down along the scabbard.

| Photo 3: front view, left hand drawing out cords | Photo 4: front view, left hand lowering cords |

Lay the sword down from here, across the front, with the hilt to the left, edge toward you.

Arrange any cords.

Bow formally.

Photo 5: front view, right hand laying sword

Photo 6: front view, *seiza*, w/ sword on ground in front

Photo 7: front view, right hand
picking up cords

Pick up any cords with the little fingers
of the right hand and stand the sword
vertically up in the center front.

Photo 8: front view, right hand
standing sword vertical

Photo 9: front view, left hand on scabbard

Grip the end of the scabbard with the left
hand.

Insert the sword into the belt as usual.

Photo 10: front view, sword inserted in *obi*

Photo 11: front view, *seiza*, inserted in *obi*

If there are cords, use the right hand to straighten them out to the right. Then tie them at the waist.

Photo 12: front view, drawing cords to right

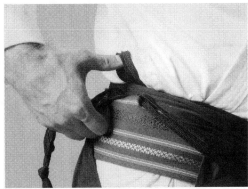

Photo 13: front closeup, tying knot

Photo 14: front closeup, tying knot

Photo 15: front view, *seiza,* w/ sword settled

Stand and move to the waiting area or directly to the practice position.

Photo 16: front view, standing, *bukezukuri*

Ending Formality

The movements of the end of practice are almost exactly the opposite of the beginning. They are identical to those of the closing formality of the All-Japan Fencing Federation Established Forms. Follow the description of the ending formality given in the previous chapter.

MAEGIRI (Front Cut)

General Description

This form is performed in the same circumstances as the *Shohatto* form in the First Tradition. The movements of the feet and knees are the same, as the enemy is struck by drawing to the front and cut down with an overhead stroke.

  The blood-cleaning used is the one prescribed for the Established Forms, that is, the *Eishin Ryu* style. The sheathing is also in the *Eishin Ryu* style.

Commentary

There is little to say about this form that has not been said earlier. The comments on Shohatto *all obtain.*

Movements

Perform the same drawing and cutting movements as are described in the *Shohatto* of the First Tradition, remembering to say "eits" on the final cut. Then, perform the following blood-cleaning and sheathing.

Demonstrating remaining heart, open the sword to the right and perform the *Eishin Ryu* blood-cleaning.

Perform the *Eishin Ryu* sheathing.
 While sheathing, pull the right foot back toward the left foot. Lower the body down onto the heels. Take a crouching posture.

Step forward with the right foot.

Stand up.

Move the left foot forward, even with the right foot.

Sit in the initial place and continue to the next form.

MAE ATOGIRI (Front-Rear Cut)

General Description

You are between two enemies, to the front and rear. Before they can strike, you fore-stall the front enemy and then attack the rear enemy. You then return and attack the front enemy. You finish the form with blood-cleaning and sheathing.

Commentary

This form requires two pivots done while kneeling. These are not simple pivots, but require you to exchange your knees. You have already seen this movement in *Tozume*, in the Inner Tradition of the Muso Shinden Ryu.

The exchange is best done by lifting the supporting knee and putting the other knee down on almost the same spot. It must be rapid and you cannot pause because of the pain.

Photo 1: front view, *seiza*, sword settled

Movements

Sit formally, facing the front.

Photo 2: front view, *seiza*,
initiating vertical draw

- Rise up on the knees.
- Draw the sword in the upper direction with a flowing parry motion.

Photo 3: front view, kneeling on both knees, draw to release

Photo 4: front view, kneeling, deflection

Place the left hand on the hilt.

Photo 5: front view, kneeling, left hand on hilt

- Advance the right foot.
- Cut downward at the front enemy.

Photo 6: front view, kneeling, downward cut

- Pivot 180-degrees to the left by raising the left knee and putting the right knee on the floor.
- Swing the sword overhead in a flowing parry motion from the right side.

Photo 7: front view, beginning turn, sword point dropping

Photo 8: front view, middle of turn, sword passing right shoulder

Photo 9: front view, kneeling, *jodan*

Photo 10: left side view, kneeling, *jodan*

Cut downward at the rear enemy's forehead.

Photo 11: front view, kneeling, downward cut

- Pivot 180 degrees to the right by raising the right knee and putting the left knee on the floor.
- Swing the sword overhead in a flowing parry motion from the left side.

Photo 12: front view, middle of turn, sword passing left shoulder

Photo 13: front view, kneeling, *jodan*

Photo 14: front view, kneeling, downward cut

Cut downward at the front enemy's forehead.

Say "eits."

Move the sword to the middle position.

Photo 15: front view, kneeling, end of *chiburi*

Perform blood-cleaning.
  Use the Eishin Ryu *style.*

Sheath.
  While sheathing, pull the right foot back and place the right knee on the floor, even with the left. The sheathing finishes the moment you are standing on both knees. Then lower the body to the sitting position.

Stand and move to the next form as before.

KIRIAGE (Rising Strike)

切
刀
り
上
げ

General Description

The enemy crowds in from the front, cutting down at you. You cut upward at his right armpit from underneath. Immediately, you cut downward from the two-handed high position in a left priest's stole cut. The form finishes with blood-cleaning and sheathing.

Commentary

This is the second of the only two forms that use the underhand draw. The first was *Kesagiri* in the previous chapter. This draw requires that you first turn the hilt and scabbard over so that the edge is down. The grip is then taken from the top of the reversed hilt, with the thumb down the side. The sword is drawn forward and upward.

The enemy has drawn and raised his sword to the high position to cut at you. The target of your underhand draw and cut is his right armpit, which is exposed in the high position.

Following this cut, you swing the sword around the left shoulder into the high position and cut down with the priest's stole cut.

A Buddhist priest's stole is a rectangle of cloth worn around the body, from the left shoulder to the right armpit. In older sword drawing terms the name of this cloth became associated with a downward diagonal cut from the top of the left shoulder (or the right) across the body.

Movements

- Advance the left foot.

- Turn the scabbard over in the belt, so that the edge faces down.

Photo 1: front view, standing, *bukezukuri*

Photo 2: front view, standing, initiating draw

Photo 3: front view, standing, underhand cut

- Advance the right foot.
- Draw the sword upward, cutting the enemy's right armpit.

- Move the left foot forward.
- Swing the sword around the left shoulder to the high position and add the left hand.

Photo 4: front view, standing, sword passing left shoulder

Photo 5: front view, standing, *jodan*

Photo 6: front view, standing, leftward slanting cut

- Advance the right foot.
- Cut downward at the top of the enemy's left shoulder in the priest's stole cut.
  Say "eits."

Return to the middle position.

Perform blood-cleaning.

Sheath the sword.
  Remain standing.

Make the left foot even with the right and move to the next form.

SHIHOGIRI (Four Direction Cut)

General Description

While walking, four enemies attack you from all sides. You respond and strike them, right, left, front and rear. You finish with the standing blood-cleaning and sheathing.

Commentary

The footwork in this form is more complicated than in the other Established Forms. It brings to mind techniques used in the Inner Tradition of the *Muso Shinden Ryu*. In fact, this form comes from the *Mizu Kamome Ryu* (Water Gull System).

There are four opponents, but there are five strikes. This is because the attack used on the enemy at the front is not considered devastating and he must be struck a second time.

Normally, the enemy at the rear would be considered the most dangerous. Some attempt might be made to forestall or hamper one of the others, but the enemy in the rear would be the one dispatched first.

This is not done in this form. Instead, the initial attack is made on the enemy to the right. The reason for this tactic is not known.

Four different cuts are used in the form, along with four different steps. These form the basis for dealing with a large number of enemies.

Movements

Photo 1: front view, standing, *bukezukuri*

Stand facing the front.

Advance the left foot.

- Advance the right foot even with the left.
- Look at the right enemy and point the right toes in his direction.
- Draw the sword upward with the right hand.

Photo 2: front view, standing,
initiating vertical draw, looking to right

Photo 3: front view, standing,
vertical draw to release, looking to right

Photo 4: front view, standing,
one hand rightward slanting cut

- Slide the right foot a little toward the right enemy.
- Cut the enemy's right shoulder with a single-handed priest's stole cut.
  Stop the cut at the height of his solar plexus.

Photo 5: front view view, standing,
sword pointing to rear

Rotate 180-degrees to the left, looking
at the left enemy.
*Leave the sword pointing at the right
enemy's chest.*

• Swing the sword overhead and add the
left hand.

Photo 6: front view, standing,
sword passing right shoulder

Photo 7: front view, standing, *jodan*

• Advance the right foot one full step
toward the left enemy.

• Cut down at the left enemy's forehead.

Photo 8: front view, standing, downward cut

Photo 9: front view, standing,
feet together, *hasso no gamae*

- Look at the front enemy.

- Pull the right foot back to the left foot.

- Draw the sword upward to the *left* eight-phase position.
  The sword guard is even with the mouth. The sword is over the left shoulder.

- Advance the right foot toward the front enemy.

- Cut the enemy's right torso in one stroke, using both hands.
  This is a horizontal cut from left to right.

Photo 10: front view, standing, leftward *do giri*

Photo 11: front view, standing,
leftward *do giri*

- Rotate 180-degrees to the left.

- Turn the blade upward and swing the sword up into the two-handed high position.

Photo 12: front view, standing,
middle of pivot

Photo 13: front, standing,
sword passing right shoulder

Photo 14: left side view, standing,
sword passing right shoulder

Photo 15: front, standing, *jodan*

Photo 16: left side view, standing, *jodan*

Cut at the rear enemy's forehead.

Photo 17: front view, standing, downward cut

Photo 18: left side view, standing,
downward cut

Photo 19: front view, standing,
sword passing left shoulder

- Rotate 180-degrees to the right.
- Swing the sword overhead.

Photo 20: front view, standing, *jodan*

Photo 21: front view, standing, downward cut

Cut downward at the front enemy's forehead.
  Say "eits."

Perform blood-cleaning.

Sheath.

KISAKIGAESHI (Returning Sword Point)

General Description

切
先
返

The enemy approaches and cuts at your forehead. Parry to the left with a slanting flowing parry. Putting the left hand on the sword, pull back and cut the enemy's head. Thrust and pierce his chest. Finish the form with blood-cleaning and sheathing.

Commentary

This is a very straight forward form. There is not much footwork. The swordwork, however, involves a gripped-blade technique you have not seen before.

Griping the blade with the left hand is thought to be an older method of dealing with close infighting situations. The fact that this form is from the Hoki Ryu (Old Official System) suggests it may predate others you have studied.

The left hand grips the blade early in the action. It adds power to a downward slash, allowing the sword to be used effectively in a close situation. An overhead cut would need more room.

The form also uses a thrust, with the left hand still gripping the blade. This is similar to the thrust used in *Soetezuki* in Chapter 7.

Movements

Advance the left foot.

Photo 1: front view, standing, *bukezukuri*

Photo 2: front view, standing,
initiating vertical draw

- Advance the right foot.
- Draw the sword overhead.
  The edge faces the rear. The point hangs down to the left, clearly protecting your head and shoulder. Use the sword blade ridge to form the flowing parry.

Photo 3: front view, standing, draw to release

Photo 4: front view, standing, deflection

Photo 5: front view, standing,
left hand moving to blade

- Immediately, grip the back of the blade with the left hand.
- Lowering the body slightly, slash downward at the enemy's head.
  The left hand comes up from underneath.

  The sword moves in a circle. The right hand comes to the right hip; the left hand stops in front of the waist. Coordinate the movements of the two hands, pushing and pulling, to get a powerful stroke.

Photo 6: front view, standing, downward slash

Photo 7: front view, standing, downward slash

Photo 8: front view, standing, thrust

- Advance the left foot.
- Thrust and pierce the enemy's chest. *Say "eits." The left hand remains on the back of the blade, coordinating with the right to thrust.*

Photo 9: front view, standing, end of *chiburi*

- Pull back the left foot.
- Release the left hand and move it to the left waist.
- Perform blood-cleaning.

Sheath.

Appendix

Headmaster Lineage and Systemic Development

HEADMASTER LINEAGE and SYSTEMIC DEVELOPMENT

Muso Shinden Ryu

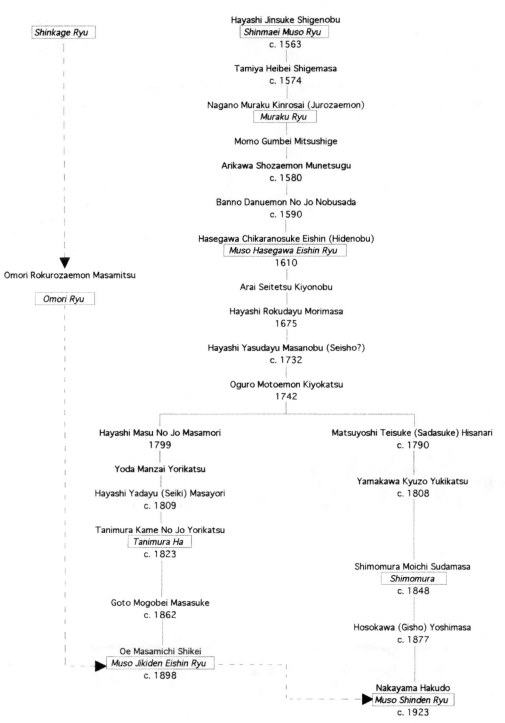

Hayashi Jinsuke Shigenobu
Shinmaei Muso Ryu
c. 1563

Tamiya Heibei Shigemasa
c. 1574

Nagano Muraku Kinrosai (Jurozaemon)
Muraku Ryu

Momo Gumbei Mitsushige

Arikawa Shozaemon Munetsugu
c. 1580

Banno Danuemon No Jo Nobusada
c. 1590

Hasegawa Chikaranosuke Eishin (Hidenobu)
Muso Hasegawa Eishin Ryu
1610

Arai Seitetsu Kiyonobu

Hayashi Rokudayu Morimasa
1675

Hayashi Yasudayu Masanobu (Seisho?)
c. 1732

Oguro Motoemon Kiyokatsu
1742

Shinkage Ryu

Omori Rokurozaemon Masamitsu

Omori Ryu

Hayashi Masu No Jo Masamori
1799

Yoda Manzai Yorikatsu

Hayashi Yadayu (Seiki) Masayori
c. 1809

Tanimura Kame No Jo Yorikatsu
Tanimura Ha
c. 1823

Goto Mogobei Masasuke
c. 1862

Oe Masamichi Shikei
Muso Jikiden Eishin Ryu
c. 1898

Matsuyoshi Teisuke (Sadasuke) Hisanari
c. 1790

Yamakawa Kyuzo Yukikatsu
c. 1808

Shimomura Moichi Sudamasa
Shimomura
c. 1848

Hosokawa (Gisho) Yoshimasa
c. 1877

Nakayama Hakudo
Muso Shinden Ryu
c. 1923

305

JAPANESE SWORD TERMS

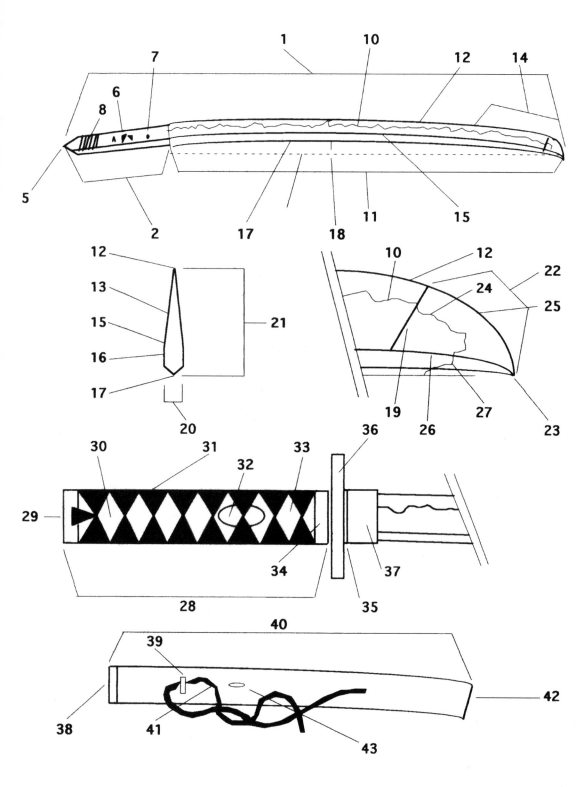

1	*To shin*	(sword blade)
2	*Nakago*	(tang)
3	*To no nagasa*	(sword length)
4	*Ha ku*	(blade section)
5	*Nakagojiri*	(tang butt)
6	*Mei*	(signature)
7	*Mekugi ana*	(rivet hole)
8	*Yasurime*	(file marks)
9	*Munelu*	(back of blade section)
10	*Hamon*	(temper pattern)
11	*Ha*	(blade)
12	*Yakiba*	(tempered edge)
13	*Ji*	(blade surface above temper pattern)
14	*Monoda*	(striking area)
15	*Shinogi*	(sword blade ridges)
16	*Shinogiji*	(blade surface above ridge line)
17	*Mune*	(back of blade)
18	*Sori*	(measure of curvature)
19	*Yokote suji*	(line dividing point from body)
20	*Omo*	(thickness)
21	*Mihaba*	(width)
22	*Mitsukado*	(triangle)
23	*Kisaki*	(point)
24	*Boshi*	(point temper pattern)
25	*Fikura*	(curve)
26	*Koshinogi*	(ridge line close to point)
27	*Kaeri*	(turning back of point temper pattern)
28	*Tsuka*	(hilt)
29	*Kashira*	(butt cap)
30	*Same*	(stingray skin)
31	*Tsukaito*	(hilt binding)
32	*Menuki*	(hilt ornaments)
33	*Mekugi*	(bamboo peg)
34	*Fuchi*	(collar)
35	*Seppa*	(washer)
36	*Tsuba*	(sword guard)
37	*Habaki*	(blade sleeve)
38	*Koiguchi*	(scabbard mouth)
39	*Kurikata*	(chord knob)
40	*Saya*	(scabbard)
41	*Sageo*	(chord)
42	*Kojiri*	(butt)
43	*Kaeshizuno*	(catch)

Glossary

Atari To
The Striking Sword; the fourth *kata* of the *Shoden* of the *Muso Shinden Ryu*

Ato
The Rear; the second *seitei kata* of the *zen nihon kendo renmei*

Boken; bokuto
A wooden practice sword

budo
The martial ways

bukezukuri
The warrior method of wearing the *katana*, through the layers of the *obi* at the left hip, edge up

---

chiburi
Blood-cleaning; a largely symbolic action of cleaning imaginary blood from the blade of the *katana*

chi nugui
Blood-wiping; a form of *chiburi*

Chuden
The Middle Tradition; the second section of *kata* within the *Muso Shinden Ryu*

Eishin Ryu
The Excellent Faith System; the style of the *kata* of the *Chuden* of the *Muso Shinden Ryu*

Eishin Ryu no chiburi
The blood-cleaning of the Excellent Faith System

eitsu
An exclamation; see, *kiai*

Ganmen Ate
Strike Between the Eyes; the eighth *seitei kata* of the *zen nihon kendo renmei*

goho giri
The five directional cut; see, *so makuri*

Gyaku To
The Reversed Sword; the eighth *kata* of the *Shoden* of the *Muso Shinden Ryu*

gyosho
The semi-cursive style; the second style of Japanese writing

---

ha
Breaking

hakama
The wide trousers worn in practice over the *juban* or *keikogi* and the *obi*

hanashi uchi
> A disengaging strike; see, *so dome*; the idiom for a strike made immediately after a parry

Hasegawa Eishin Ryu
> The Deep River Valley Excellent Faith System; the style of *kata* of the *Chuden* of the *Muso Shinden Ryu*

hidari
> The left; see, *sa to*

hitonaka
> In public; see, *kabe zoi*

Hoki Ryu
> The Old Official System

---

iaido
> The way of Japanese sword drawing

iai goshi
> The sword drawing waist; a half-standing, half-kneeling posture used in the *kata*

iaito
> A metal practice sword, without an edge

i hyoshi no uchi
> The strike of one rhythm; the idiom for the flowing motion from the vertical draw to the vertical cut

Inazuma
> Lightning; the third *kata* of the *Chuden* of the *Muso Shinden Ryu*

Inyo Shintai
> Advancing-Retreating Movement; the fifth *kata* of the *Shoden* of the *Muso Shinden Ryu*

Inyo Shintai Kaewaza
> The Advancing-Retreating Movement, Alternate Technique; the twelfth, and alternate *kata* of the *Shoden* of the *Muso Shinden Ryu*

Itomagoi
> Farewell Visit; the twenty-first *kata* of the *Okuden* of the *Muso Shinden Ryu*

Iwanami
> Waves Breaking Against Rocks; the sixth *kata* of the *Chuden* of the *Muso Shinden Ryu*

---

juban
> A short upper undergarment

Jun To
> The Obedient Sword; the seventh *kata* of the *Shoden* of the *Muso Shinden Ryu*

Kabe Zoi
> Adjusting for the Wall; the seventeenth *kata* of the *Okuden* of the *Muso Shinden Ryu*

kaishaku
> The assistant at the formal Japanese suicide ceremony; see, *junto*

kaisho

The printed style; the first style of Japanese writing

kakure sute

Hide and discard; see, *mon iri*

Kasumi

Mist; the first *kata* of the *Okuden* of the *Muso Shinden Ryu*

kata

The forms of any Japanese martial or cultural art

katana

A Japanese sword, of the later, shorter length, designed to be worn in the *bukezukuri* fashion

katsugi

To carry on the shoulder

keikogi

A short upper practice garment, heavier than a *juban*

kendo

The way of Japanese fencing

ken no koto

Circumstantial wisdom; see, *sodesurigaeshi*

kesagiri

The priest's stole cut; a downward slanting cut, usually directed at one of the shoulders; also, the Priest's Stole Cut; the fifth *seitei kata* of the *zen nihon kendo renmei*

kiai

A spirit meeting; the idiom for a shout given in company with an aggressive move

Kiriage

The Rising Strike; the third *seitei kata* of the *zen nihon iaido renmei*

kiri tsuke

Cutting with the *katana*

Kisakigaeshi

The Returning Sword Point; the fifth *seitei kata* of the *zen nihon iaido renmei*

Koran To

The Tiger-Fighting Sword; the tenth *kata* of the *Shoden* of the *Muso Shinden Ryu*

Mae

The front; see, *shohatto*; also, the first *seitei kata* of the *zen nihon kendo renmei*

Mae Atogiri

The Front-Rear Cut; the second *seitei kata* of the *zen nihon iaido renmei*

Maegiri

The Front Cut; the first *seitei kata* of the *zen nihon iaido renmei*

mae muki

Facing the front; see, *morote zuki*

maai
> Meeting space; the idiom
> for the proper distance
> for an effective attack

migi
> The right; see, *u to*

migi muki
> Facing the right; see,
> *ukenagashi*

mi sumi
> Three corners; see, *tozume*

Mizu Kamome Ryu
> The Water Gull System

Mon Iri
> Entering the Gate; the six-
> teenth *kata* of the *Okuden*
> of the *Muso Shinden Ryu*

Morote Zuki
> The Two-Handed Thrust;
> the sixth *seitei kata* of the
> *zen nihon kendo renmei*

Mugai Ryu
> The Nothing Excluded System

muko barai
> Beating the other; see, *kasumi*

muko zume
> The other enclosed; see, *towaki*

musei no kiai
> The soundless spirit meeting;
> the idiom for the quite per-
> formance of the *kata* of the
> *Okuden* of the *Muso Shinden
> Ryu*

Muso Shinden Ryu
> The Traditional Spiritual Vision
> System of *iaido*

Namigaeshi
> Returning Waves; the eighth
> *kata* of the *Chuden* of the *Muso
> Shinden Ryu*

noto
> Sheathing the *katana*

nuki tsuke
> Drawing the *katana* in the
> horizontal manner

Nuki Uchi
> Sudden Attack; the eleventh
> *kata* of the *Shoden* of the *Muso
> Shinden Ryu*; the tenth *kata*
> of the *Chuden* of the *Muso
> Shinden Ryu*; see, *kesagiri*

---

obi
> A wide belt used to close the
> *juban* or *keikogi*

Oikakegiri
> Pursuing Cut; the nineteenth
> *kata* of the *Okuden* of the
> *Muso Shinden Ryu*

oikaze
> Pursuing wind; see, *koran to*

Okuden
> The Inner Tradition; the third
> section of *kata* within the *Muso
> Shinden Ryu*

Omori Ryu
> The Big Forest System; the
> style of *kata* in the *Shoden*
> of the *Muso Shinden Ryu*

Omori Ryu no chiburi
> The blood-cleaning of the
> *Omori Ryu.*

renmei

A federated organization of any Japanese martial or cultural arts

ri

Leaving

Ryoshi Hikitsure "ryoshi hikit sre"
Both Warriors Brought Together; the twentieth *kata* of the *Okuden* of the *Muso Shinden Ryu*

Ryozume

Both Enclosed; the seventh *kata* of the *Okuden* of the *Muso Shinden Ryu*

ryu

Any system of Japanese martial or cultural arts

Ryu To

The Flowing Sword; the sixth *kata* of the *Shoden* of the *Muso Shinden Ryu*

---

sagi ashi

The legs of a heron; the idiom for a one-legged stance in which the shins cross

sammen o muki

Facing three centers; see, *sanpogiri*

Sanpogiri

Three Directional Cut; the seventh *seitei kata* of the *zen nihon kendo renmei*

Sa To

The Following Sword; the second *kata* of the *Shoden* of the *Muso Shinden Ryu*

Seichu To

The Center-Strengthened Sword; the ninth *kata* of the *Shoden* of the *Muso Shinden Ryu*

seitei kata

The established *kata* of a *renmei*

seiza

The formal seated position

seme

Attacking

seppuku

The formal Japanese suicide ceremony

Shihogiri

The Four Directional Cut; the third *kata* of the *Okuden* of the *Muso Shinden Ryu* ; also, The Four Directional Cut; the fourth *seitei kata* of the *zen nihon iaido renmei* ; also, The Four Directional Cut; the tenth *seitei kata* of the *zen nihon kendo renmei*

Shingaku An

The Hermitage of Self-Study

Shinobu

The Faithful Husband; the thirteenth *kata* of the *Okuden* of the *Muso Shinden Ryu*

Shinto Munen Ryu
> The Way of the Gods and the
> Impassive Mind System

shi sumi
> Four corners; see, *shihogiri*

Shoden
> The First Tradition; the first
> section of *kata* within the *Muso
> Shinden Ryu*

Shohatto
> The Initial Sword; the first *kata*
> of the *Shoden* of the *Muso
> Shinden Ryu*

shomen
> The center; see, *mae* ; see,
> *tsuka ate*

shomen muki
> Facing the center, see, *kesagiri*

shu
> Keeping

Sodesurigaeshi
> Returning from Brushing the
> Sleeve; the fifteenth *kata* of the
> *Okuden* of the *Muso Shinden
> Ryu*

So Dome
> All Stopped; the twelfth *kata* of
> the *Okuden* of the *Muso
> Shinden Ryu*

Soetezuki
> Fixing Thrust; the ninth *seitei
> kata* of the *zen nihon kendo
> renmei*

So Makuri
> All Rolled Up; the eleventh
> *kata* of the *Okuden* of the
> *Muso Shinden Ryu*

sosho
> The cursive style; the third
> style of Japanese writing

sui hashiri
> Running water; the idiom for
> the slight angle of the blade at
> the end of the horizontal draw

suihei osame to
> The horizontally stopping
> sword; the idiom for the angle
> the blade finally assumes in
> the *Eishin Ryu no chiburi*

Sunegakoi
> Enclosed Shin; the second
> *kata* of the *Okuden* of the
> *Muso Shinden Ryu*

Taki Otoshi
> Dropping Waterfall; the ninth
> *kata* of the *Chuden* of the
> *Muso Shinden Ryu*

Tanashita
> The Lower Shelf; the sixth *kata*
> of the *Okuden* of the *Muso
> Shinden Ryu*

tate hiza
> The drawn-up knee position;
> a sitting position used in the
> advanced *kata*

to o furi kamuri
> Swinging the sword overhead;
> the idiom for the circular pass-
> ing of the blade around the left
> shoulder into a two-handed,
> overhead position

Tora Bashiri
> Rushing Tiger; the eighth *kata*
> of the *Okuden* of the *Muso
> Shinden Ryu*

Tora Issoku
Pair of Tigers; the second *kata* of the *Chuden* of the *Muso Shinden Ryu*

Towaki
Side Door; the fifth *kata* of the *Okuden* of the *Muso Shinden Ryu*

Tozume
Enclosing Doors; the fourth *kata* of the *Okuden* of the *Muso Shinden Ryu*

Tsuka Ate
The Hilt Strike; the fourth *seitei kata* of the *zen nihon kendo renmei*

tsuka dome
Hilt stop; see, *sunegakoi*

tsukekomi
The idiom for taking advantage; see, *gyaku to*

tsukikage
Moonlight; see, *seichu to*

Tsuredachi
Together; the tenth *kata* of the *Okuden* of the *Muso Shinden Ryu*

Ukenagashi
Parrying; see, *ryu to* ; the idiom for the deflection of the opponent's blade over the left shoulder; also, Flowing Parry; the eighteenth *kata* of the *Okuden* of the *Muso Shinden Ryu* ; also, The Flowing Parry; the third *seitei kata* of the *zen nihon kendo renmei*

Ukigumo
Floating Clouds; the fourth *kata* of the *Chuden* of the *Muso Shinden Ryu*

Urokogaeshi
Returning Pattern; the seventh *kata* of the *Chuden* of the *Muso Shinden Ryu*

ushiro
The rear; see, *atari to*

ushiro muki
Facing the rear; see, *ato*

U To
The Right Sword; the third *kata* of the *Shoden* of the *Muso Shinden Ryu*

---

yae gaki
Doubled fences; see, *inyo shintai*

yakuza no osame to
The gambler's sheathing style

Yamaoroshi
Mountain Wind; the fifth *kata* of the *Chuden* of the *Muso Shinden Ryu*

Yokogumo
Bank of Clouds; the first *kata* of the *Chuden* of the *Muso Shinden Ryu*

yorumi nuki
The relaxed draw; see, *ukenagashi*

yoru no tachi
The long sword in the night; see, *shinobu*

Yukichigai
> Crossing; the fourteenth *kata* of the *Okuden* of the *Muso Shinden Ryu*

Yuki Tsure
> Accompanying; the ninth *kata* of the *Okuden* of the *Muso Shinden Ryu*

zan shin
> Remaining heart; the idiom for the conscious, alert state following the conclusion of any action

---

Zen Nihon Iaido Renmei
> The All-Japan Sword Drawing Federation

Zen Nihon Kendo Renmei
> The All-Japan Fencing Federation

PARTICIPANTS' STATEMENTS

L to r: Rich Radcliffe, Don Zier, Tom Lang

AUTHOR: DON J. ZIER

Japanese martial arts are infused with Japanese culture; they do not exist in a vacuum, easily transported to another society. As American students, we must be aware of the legacy of Japanese culture that comes with the arts. However, we have our own legacy, too, and we must also take into account the heritage of western culture we bring to our study.

During my involvement in the martial arts I have tried to balance two forces: the Eastern, mystical martial arts themselves, and the Western, rationalist disciplines of study and analysis. The first brings us Japanese traditions and techniques. We bring the second with us to class, a unique set of learning tools we can apply to gain new perspective and mastery.

My study of the Japanese martial disciplines began in the 1950s with body arts (Judo and Aikido) and moved to weapons systems (Jodo and Iaido and, in the 1980s, to Kyudo). My active practice was cut short in 1988 when I was struck by an automobile. Subsequent to the writing of this book, further complications have forced me to retire from the martial arts altogether.

I wish to thank my students, Tom Lang and Richard Radcliffe, who posed for most of the photographs in this work to illustrate techniques I am no longer able to do.

Demonstrator: Tom Lang

I began practicing the martial arts in 1971. I hold a fourth-degree black belt in Danzan Ryu (Kodenkan) Jujitsu from the American Judo and Jujitsu Federation and a second-degree black belt in Muso Shinden Ryu Iaido from the All Japan Kendo Federation. I have also trained for many years in the Filipino martial arts, especially Kali, and in Bokendo, a martial art employing a heavy, curved, wooden staff in the manner of a riot baton, taught within Danzan Ryu Jujitsu. I have studied Iaido, the four-foot staff (jo), and the spear (yari) with Don Zier since 1975 and am co-author with him of *The Japanese Short Staff*, a book on the jo, also published by Unique Publications.

Demonstrator: Rich Radcliffe

I have studied several martial arts, both Chinese and Japanese, with various instructors. I began the study of Dan Zan Ryu Jujitsu in 1970 and hold a fourth-degree rank. I have studied Iaido with Don Zier since 1975, and have run my own dojo for many years.